D1526764

Godfathers and Cybersecurity: A Gangster's Take on Cybersecurity

By Lance Harris

First paperback and hardcover editions October 2024

Book design by Lance Harris
All figures and art created with Midjourney.com

ISBN 9798862504613 (paperback)
ISBN 9798340923929 (hardcover)
Independently published

DEDICATION

To all my brothers and sisters in arms, fighting to stay
one step ahead of the bad guys.

TABLE OF CONTENTS

Introduction

Readers,

Thank you for picking up a copy of *Godfathers and Cybersecurity*. This was a fun book to write. I hope it will be a fun read and you learn a few things along the way. I certainly learned a few things pulling it together. I found that the lessons and stories really came to life through the voice of a 1930s gangster. There's a certain gravitas and tone that only a gangster could bring to the narrative.

So, without further ado, I hand it over to Vinnie to be your guide.

Have fun,
Lance

Alright, folks, grab a seat and listen close, 'cause Vinnie "the Squid" Marconi is here with somethin' important to spill. What you're holding in your hands ain't just a book, it's a roadmap to survive and thrive in a world that's become just as cutthroat and unpredictable as the streets I used to run. In *Godfathers and Cybersecurity*, you're not just going to get a peek behind the curtain of the mob; you're getting a front-row seat to the biggest heists, backstabs, and takedowns in cyber history, delivered through the eyes of someone who knows a thing or two about staying ahead of the competition.

This ain't your run-of-the-mill cybersecurity manual; this is street wisdom applied to the digital age. And if you think the mob was ruthless, wait 'til you see what hackers and cybercriminals are doing today. From ransomware attacks to large-scale breaches, they're playing the same game we played in the alleyways, just with different tools. If you're reading this, you're about to learn how those street smarts can help you stay one step ahead in the cyber world.

Chapter Highlights:

Chapter 1: A Kind Word and a Digital Gun

Just like Al Capone once said, "You can get further with a kind word and a gun than with just a kind word." In the digital world, that "gun" is ransomware, malware, and brute-force hacks. You'll learn how cybercriminals blend charm and intimidation, using social engineering to crack systems wide open, just like the smooth-talking gangsters of old.

Chapter 2: Don't Keep All Your Eggs in One Basket

Back in the day, we didn't trust just one safe house or one stash spot. The same rule applies to your data and systems today. In this chapter, we break down how to spread your risks and stay nimble, just like Meyer Lansky did when running his gambling empire. Cybersecurity isn't about locking one door; it's about having multiple exits ready when things go south.

Chapter 3: Everyone's Got a Plan Until They Get Punched in the Mouth

Mike Tyson might've coined that phrase, but Bugsy Siegel lived it. The rise and fall of mobsters is mirrored in some of the biggest cyber disasters. Learn how some of the most infamous hacks, like the

SolarWinds attack, threw companies and governments into chaos, just like a well-placed punch that sends plans tumbling.

Chapter 4: All I Do is Supply a Demand

Al Capone didn't create Prohibition, but he sure as hell profited from it. The same goes for the rise of ransomware and zero-day exploits. In this chapter, you'll see how hackers today are capitalizing on the underground demand for data, exploits, and vulnerabilities, and why this black market is booming like the bootlegging operations of old.

Chapter 5: Trust is Good, But Control is Better, See?

In both the streets and the cyber realm, trust is a currency more valuable than cash, but control is the ultimate prize. Just like the mob-controlled unions and entire industries, modern hackers are all about controlling information. Learn how breaches like the Facebook–Cambridge Analytica scandal taught us that sometimes it's not enough to have access, you need total control.

Chapter 7: This is Nothing Personal, It's Strictly Business

The line between personal and business is razor-thin when you're running a crime family or a cybercrime syndicate. This chapter delves into the cold, calculated moves of both cyber criminals and real-life mob bosses, showing how manipulation, exploitation, and leverage drive the underworld and the digital battleground alike.

Chapter 9: Don't Let Anyone Know What You're Thinking

The Mafia lived by a code of silence, Omertà. The same principle applies in cybersecurity: the less you give away, the better your chances of surviving. Learn from real-world examples like the Apple-FBI tango, where keeping secrets meant everything.

Chapter 10: Never Sell What You Love

Some things, like loyalty and principles, should never be for sale. This chapter explores how digital crooks often sell themselves short, taking risks for short-term gains. We'll also look at how some companies sold out their security for convenience and paid the ultimate price.

Chapter 11: You'll Never Take Me Alive, Copper!

Ransomware-as-a-Service (RaaS) lets anyone hire hackers, just like renting muscle. DDoS attacks overwhelm websites like a mob storming a rival's spot. Cyber extortion is the modern protection racket, demanding payment to unlock systems. The Silk Road reflects black-market deals, while untraceable money laundering through cryptocurrency hides illegal cash flows. Though the tools are digital now, the game of intimidation and profit remains the same.

So, Why This Book?

Because the cyber world is just as treacherous as the mob's heyday, and in both worlds, the rules are simple: stay smart, stay sharp, and always watch your back. The lessons you'll pick up here are time-tested, battle-worn, and straight from the mouths of the most cunning gangsters, applied to the digital battlefield.

Think you're ready? Capisce? Then let's dive in, and may you walk away from this book a little wiser, a little tougher, and a whole lot more prepared for what the cyber world has waiting for you.
Now, let's get down to business, shall we?

Chapter 1: A Kind Word and a Digital Gun

Hey there, pal! Pull up a chair, pour yourself a drink, and let ol' Vinnie "the Squid" Marconi give you the lowdown on this whole cybersecurity shebang. Now, I ain't no tech whiz, but I've been around the block a few times, and lemme tell ya, the streets of Chicago in the '30s ain't so different from this digital jungle you folks navigate today.

You ever hear of Big Al? Al Capone? Of course, you have! The man was a genius, a visionary. He once said, "You can get much farther with a kind word and a gun than you can with a kind word alone." Now, I've lived by that motto my whole life, and it's served me well in the speakeasies, the poker tables, and the back alleys. But you might be scratchin' your noggin, wondering, "Vinnie, what's that got to do with computers and the interwebs?"

Well, let me break it down for ya, see?

In our world, the "kind word" was the charm, the charisma, the ability to sweet-talk your way into or out of any situation. In your digital age, that's what they call "social engineering." It's the art of manipulating folks into giving up confidential information. Maybe it's pretending to be someone you ain't, or maybe it's just buttering someone up real nice-like. Either way, it's all about the gift of gab.

But sometimes, talk ain't enough. That's where the "gun" comes in. Now, I ain't talking about a Tommy gun or a snub-nose .38. In the world of cybersecurity, your "gun" is that nasty piece of code, that malware or ransomware, that gives you the upper hand. It's the threat that backs up your sweet words, the muscle that makes sure folks take you seriously.

Is that a pistol in ya pocket? (Midjourney, 2023)

You see, when you combine that charm with a real, tangible threat, you become unstoppable. It's like walking into a joint with a smile and a pistol in your belt. Everyone's all smiles back, but they know, deep down, that you mean business. And in the digital realm, that business can be anything from stealing sensitive data to locking up entire systems until a hefty ransom is paid.

See here, I got a couple o' examples for ya..

1. The Twitter Bitcoin Scam (2020)

Ah, let's take a trip down recent memory lane, shall we? Remember that big hullabaloo in 2020 when some of the biggest names on Twitter, like Joe Biden, Elon Musk, and even ol' Billy Gates, started tweeting out about giving away Bitcoin? (BBC, 2020)

We're talkin' about the Twitter Bitcoin Scam of 2020, a modern-day heist that would've made even Al Capone tip his hat. Now, that was a classic case of using a "kind word" backed by a digital "gun."

The Kind Word: A Digital Masquerade

Imagine waking up, scrolling through your Twitter feed, and seeing Elon Musk or Joe Biden offering to double your Bitcoin. Sounds too good to be true, right? Well, that's the "kind word" part of the equation. These hackers used the social capital and trust built up by these high-profile figures to lure people into their trap. It was like offering free booze during Prohibition; people couldn't resist.

The Art of Persuasion

The hackers knew that a message from a trusted source would be far more effective than some random account. They leveraged the credibility of these public figures to give their scam an air of legitimacy. It throws people off the scent, the digital equivalent of a mobster being a pillar of the community.

The Digital Gun: A Masterclass in Social Engineering

Now, here's where the "gun" comes into play. These weren't just some run-of-the-mill hackers. They were artists of deception. They managed to manipulate Twitter employees into granting them access to internal systems. Once inside, they had the keys to the digital gun locker to impersonate the trusted high-profile individuals.

The Muscle Behind the Operation

With control over these high-profile accounts, the hackers could send out their "kind words" with the force of a digital Tommy gun. They had the power to make or break reputations, to sway public opinion, and most importantly, to empty pockets.

The Heist and the Fallout

Before anyone knew what hit 'em, these modern-day gangsters had made off with over $100,000 in Bitcoin. Sure, it's not Fort Knox, but for a few hours of work, it ain't bad. And just like any good heist, the planning and execution were impeccable, but it was the combination of great offer ("the kind word") and the trust of using the high-profile users accounts ("the gun") that made it all possible.

Lessons Learned:

- **The Power of Credibility**: These hackers didn't just hack any old accounts; they went for the big names like Musk, Biden, Gates. Why? Because people trust 'em. When you've got credibility, people are more likely to fall for your schemes. **Lesson**: In both crime and cybersecurity, it's all about trust. Whether you're runnin' a con or a legit operation, credibility gets people on your side. Guard it carefully.

- **The Art of Manipulation**: The hackers didn't break in through some fancy technical trick. Nah, they sweet-talked their way in by manipulating Twitter employees. That's the beauty of social engineering. It's not about bustin' through the front

door; it's about convincin' someone to leave it open.
Lesson: In cybersecurity, the weakest link is often the person, not the system. Manipulating people is just as dangerous as crackin' passwords.

- **The Importance of Access**: Once these hackers got inside, they had the keys to the kingdom. With access to the right accounts, they could impersonate some of the most trusted folks on the planet. It's like gettin' the combination to the boss's safe.
  Lesson: It ain't just about breakin' in; it's about where you break in. If you get access to the right tools or people, you can pull off any job, digital or otherwise.

- **The Combination is Key**: A kind word will open some doors, sure. But if you back it up with muscle (or in this case, control over trusted accounts), you can make a killing. The hackers knew that charm wasn't enough. They needed a gun, and Twitter's internal system was that gun.
  Lesson: A slick plan ain't worth much without the muscle to back it up. In cybersecurity, you need both strategy and brute force defense to protect what's yours.

Cybersecurity Relevance: So, kid, this Twitter Bitcoin caper from 2020? It's a modern-day shakedown, see? These hackers used the trust of some big names, like Biden and Musk, to sweet-talk the public into coughing up their Bitcoin. In the cyber world, that's social engineering at its finest, playing on trust to make a quick score. Just like back in the day when you used a charming front to pull off a heist. When it comes to cybersecurity, trust ain't enough, ya gotta protect those systems with more than just a smile and handshake.

So, the next time you think about cybersecurity, remember this tale. It's not just about firewalls and antivirus software; it's about understanding human psychology and behavior. After all, you can get much farther with a kind word and a gun than you can with a kind word alone.

2. The WannaCry Ransomware Attack (2017)

Gather 'round, folks! Let me tell ya about a tale that's as chilling as a Chicago winter. We're talkin' about the WannaCry Ransomware Attack of 2017, a digital shakedown that would've made even the toughest mobsters of my day say, "Hey, that's some operation you got there!" (Wikipedia, n.d.)

The Kind Word: A Polite Extortion Note

Picture this: You're sittin' at your desk, minding your own business, and then BAM! your computer screen changes. You're greeted with a message that's almost polite, like a gentleman gangster from the '30s. It tells you that your files are locked up tighter than Alcatraz but offers you a way out. Pay up in Bitcoin, and you'll get your precious data back. There's even a countdown timer, adding a sense of urgency, like a ticking time bomb.

The message is crafted to be as user-friendly as a ransom note can be. It provided step-by-step instructions on how to make the payment, almost like a customer service rep guiding you through a transaction. It's the kind word that makes you think, "Well, they're not so bad; they're giving me a way out."

The Gun: Ransomware

Now, here's where the "gun" comes in. This isn't just a simple piece of malware; it is a full-blown ransomware attack that exploits a vulnerability in Windows. Once it gets into a system, it spreads like gossip in a speakeasy, locking up files and holding them hostage.

The ransomware itself is the muscle, the firepower. It doesn't just lock up a single computer; it targets entire networks. Hospitals, factories, schools, you name it. It is like a gangster walking into a store, breaking a few windows, and then saying, "Nice place you got here; it'd be a shame if something happened to it."

The Aftermath: A Global Shakedown

By the time the authorities got a handle on this digital crime wave, WannaCry had hit over 200,000 computers across 150 countries, causing billions in damages. It was a global operation, the likes of which even the most ambitious mobsters of yesteryears could only dream of. (Fruhlinger, 2022)

Lessons Learned:

- **The Art of Persuasion**: WannaCry wasn't just about brute force; it came with a nice, polite ransom note, offering a way out. That's the con at its finest. Make 'em think you're giving 'em an option when there's really no choice.
  Lesson: Whether you're a gangster or a hacker, knowing how to sweet-talk your victim is key. In cybersecurity, those "polite" messages in phishing emails and ransomware are just part of the act. Don't fall for it.

- **The Power of Leverage**: This attack wasn't just about sending out a threat. It had the muscle to back it up. Once that ransomware hit, it spread fast and hard, locking up systems across entire networks. That's the equivalent of walking into a shop with a Tommy gun.
  Lesson: In cybersecurity, the leverage comes from the threat of locked-up data. Always remember, your files are valuable. If you're not protected, one breach, and it's all over.

- **The Scale of Operations**: Back in the day, a small crew could take over a block, maybe a whole neighborhood. But these hackers? They pulled off a global operation, hitting 200,000 computers in 150 countries. That's taking crime to a whole new level.

Lesson: In today's digital world, a small group of hackers can have an impact on a global scale. Cybersecurity needs to be just as global and prepared to face these widespread attacks.

- **The Importance of Preparedness**: Back in the old days, businesses paid the mob for protection to avoid trouble. Today, companies need to be investing in cybersecurity, backups, and disaster recovery plans to avoid getting hit by digital gangsters.
  Lesson: Don't wait until the attack happens. Be prepared. Have your systems backed up, and make sure your security measures are up to date, or you'll be payin' the ransom and wishin' you'd planned ahead.

Cybersecurity Relevance: This WannaCry business? That was a global shakedown on a scale Al Capone could only dream of. These hackers didn't need a Tommy gun. They had ransomware, locking up data like it was gold in a safe. Pay the ransom, or your files stay locked up tighter than Fort Knox. The lesson for you today, pal, is that in cybersecurity, you need more than firewalls. You gotta be prepared with backups and disaster recovery plans, 'cause trust me, the muscle these hackers pack? It's digital, but just as dangerous.

So, there you go kid. The game's the same; only the players have changed. Whether you're running a numbers racket or a global ransomware campaign, the principles hold true. A kind word can get you far, but a kind word backed by a gun? Well, that can get you anywhere.

Here's a couple more for ya, kid.

3. The St. Valentine's Day Massacre (1929)

Let's take a trip back in time, shall we? To the days of speakeasies, jazz, and the kind of gangster action that makes modern-day shenanigans look like child's play. I'm talkin' about the St. Valentine's Day Massacre of 1929, a day that left a bloody mark on the Windy City and perfectly encapsulates Big Al's philosophy of mixing charm with a little bit of firepower. (Eig, 2010)

The Kind Word: A Deceptive Setup

Picture it: A cold February morning in Chicago. Four men walk into a garage at 2122 North Clark Street. Two of 'em are dressed as cops, see? The seven guys inside, all part of Bugs Moran's crew, think it's just another shakedown by the boys in blue. They line up against the wall, expecting the usual pat-down and maybe a confiscation of some bootlegged booze.

The uniformed "cops" played their roles to perfection. They had the posture, the demeanor, and the authority that comes with a badge. To the Moran gang, it was a routine inconvenience, a temporary hiccup in their daily operations. They had no reason to suspect that they were walking into a death trap.

The Gun - Real Guns

Just when the Moran gang thought they were in for a routine police search, the tables turned. The two "cops" and their two accomplices whipped out Tommy guns and let 'em rip. It was a hailstorm of lead, and when the smoke cleared, all seven men were dead, riddled with bullets.

This wasn't just a random act of violence; it was a calculated move in the ongoing turf war between Al Capone's South Side gang and Bugs Moran's North Side crew. The Tommy guns were the muscle, the show of force that sent a clear message: Capone's gang was not to be trifled with.

The Aftermath: An Unsolved Mystery

Despite the brutality and the audacity of the attack, nobody was ever convicted. Capone, the suspected mastermind, had a rock-solid alibi. He was in Florida, far away from the bloody streets of Chicago. The massacre was believed to be the culmination of a power struggle between the South Side Italian gang led by Al Capone and the North Side Irish gang led by Bugs Moran. While Capone was widely suspected of ordering the hit, he was never charged, and the crime remains officially unsolved. (Eig, 2010)

Lessons Learned:

- **The Element of Surprise**: Those Moran boys thought they were just getting shaken down by the cops, but they walked into an ambush. The surprise attack caught 'em off guard, sealing their fate.
  Lesson: In cybersecurity, just like in the streets, catching your target off guard is key. Whether it's through a phishing email or a sneaky malware attack, the element of surprise can cripple even the toughest defenses.

- **The Use of Force**: Capone's crew didn't just stroll in. They brought Tommy guns, and boy, did they use 'em. When you're sendin' a message, sometimes you need to bring the muscle.
  Lesson: In the cyber world, the "muscle" is ransomware or a DDoS attack. Sometimes hackers use brute force, and if your defenses aren't strong enough, you're gonna get taken down hard.

- **The Importance of Planning**: This massacre wasn't a spur-of-the-moment job. It was planned down to the last detail. Capone's boys posed as cops, caught the enemy off guard, and pulled off the perfect hit.
  Lesson: Cyberattacks are no different. The best ones are planned meticulously, with hackers knowing exactly when and where to strike. If you don't have a plan in place for your own defense, you're asking for trouble.

- **The Impunity of Power**: Capone had an ironclad alibi, sipping cocktails in Florida while his enemies were getting ventilated in Chicago. No matter what happened, the law couldn't pin it on him.
  Lesson: Modern hackers can operate with the same kind of impunity, hiding in countries with lax cybersecurity laws. They can pull off a massive cyber hit and walk away scot-free, just like Capone did.

- **The Legacy of Violence**: The St. Valentine's Day Massacre wasn't just another killing. It shook the entire city and changed how the law went after organized crime.
  Lesson: Major cyberattacks have lasting impacts, too. WannaCry, SolarWinds, or other major hits force companies and governments to rethink their strategies and beef up their defenses.

Cybersecurity Relevance: Now, this here massacre was all about planning, surprise, and sheer muscle. The kind of muscle these cyber goons use today ain't bullets, but malware. They creep in, posing as the good guys, just like those fake cops in Chicago, and before you know it, bam! Your whole operation's wiped out. In cybersecurity, you need to plan like Capone. Be ready for anything and strike back fast, or your network will be riddled with holes, just like Moran's boys.

There you have it. A kind word might get you through the door, but if you really want to make an impact, you'll need a gun or in today's terms, some serious hacking skills. It's a lesson as old as time, just dressed up in different clothes.

4. The Fixing of the 1919 World Series (Black Sox Scandal)

Baseball, America's pastime! But let me tell ya, not everything is peanuts and Cracker Jacks in the world of sports. Take the 1919

World Series, for instance. It's a tale that's got more twists and turns than a back alley in Chicago, and it perfectly illustrates the idea that a kind word can get you far, but a kind word with a gun? Well, that's a home run, baby! (Andrews, 2023)

The Kind Word: The Allure of Easy Money

Picture it: Eight players from the Chicago White Sox, some of the best in the game, get a proposition they can't easily refuse. Throw the World Series against the Cincinnati Reds, and they'd be rolling in dough. For guys who felt like they were getting the short end of the stick from their team owner, this was an offer that seemed too good to pass up.

The gamblers who approached the players knew exactly what strings to pull. They talked about the unfairness of the baseball system, the low salaries, and the lack of recognition. They offered a way out, a chance to get what the players felt they deserved. It was a kind word, a promise of better days, and for a moment, it seemed like everyone would get what they wanted.

The Gun: Threat to Their Lives

But let's not forget who we're dealing with here. Behind the scenes were some heavy hitters in the gambling world, including the infamous Arnold Rothstein. These guys weren't just businessmen; they were gangsters. And gangsters play for keeps.

While the initial offer was wrapped in the allure of easy money, the players knew there was an unspoken threat hanging in the air. Cross these guys, and you'd find yourself in a world of hurt. It wasn't just about the money; it was about the power and the fear that came with it. The players knew that if they didn't play ball—literally—they'd be facing more than a tarnished reputation. They'd be risking their lives.

The Aftermath: A Scandal for the Ages

When the scheme was eventually uncovered, the fallout was catastrophic. Eight players, some of whom could have been among the greatest to ever play the game, were banned for life. The scandal shook the nation and changed the face of baseball forever.

Lessons Learned:

- **The Power of Persuasion**: The gamblers knew how to talk sweet, offering easy money to those White Sox players like it was a dream deal. They knew just what to say to get 'em hooked.
  Lesson: In the cyber world, the first move in a scam is all about making it look like an opportunity you can't refuse. Phishing schemes and insider threats work just the same, bait 'em with promises, then reel 'em in.

- **The Threat of Force**: Behind the kind words, there was muscle, like Arnold Rothstein, who weren't afraid to lay down the law. Sure, the deal looked good, but everyone knew that if they didn't play along, they'd be in big trouble.
  Lesson: In cybersecurity, the threat isn't always in your face. Sometimes it's what's not said, like ransomware attacks or blackmail. Hackers let you know they have the upper hand, and if you don't play by their rules, you'll face the consequences.

- **The Consequences of Choices**: Those eight players thought they were making a smart move, but in the end, it cost them their careers and their legacy. Banned for life.
  Lesson: In the digital game, one wrong move, like falling for a phishing scam or ignoring security protocols can lead to a major breach that destroys careers and reputations. Be careful, because there are no do-overs.

- **The Complexity of Motivation**: These players weren't just motivated by greed; they felt underpaid and underappreciated. It wasn't just about the money; it was about sticking it to the system.
  Lesson: People make bad decisions for all kinds of reasons. In cybersecurity, this is where insider threats come in. Employees feeling underpaid or overlooked might be more tempted to compromise security for a quick payout.

- **The Unpredictability of Outcomes**: The fix seemed perfect, but like any well-laid plan, it fell apart. The truth came out, and the scandal rocked the nation.
  Lesson: Even the slickest cyberattacks can unravel. No matter how carefully a scheme is planned, the truth tends to come out. Hackers and insider threats may think they're in the clear, but there's always a risk that their crimes will catch up with them.

Cybersecurity Relevance: Now, this one's a tale of easy money and dirty tricks. Just like the Sox threw the game for cash, today's hackers rig the system for a quick payday. In the cyber world, the allure of easy money leads to insider threats, phishing schemes, and backdoor deals. What's the takeaway? Don't let greed or shortcuts ruin your game, and always have your eyes on the field. One wrong move in cybersecurity, and you may be out of the game, banned for life.
A kind word might open doors, but when you back it up with the power of intimidation, well, you can swing for the fences. Just remember, every choice has its consequences, and sometimes, you strike out.

These tales highlight the potent combination of persuasion and threat. Whether it's the allure of easy money or the fear of violent reprisal, the tactics remain timeless. It's all about getting what you want, by any means necessary.

Now, I ain't condoning any of this, mind you. I'm just drawing parallels between our world and yours. But if there's one thing I've learned from my time running with the big dogs, it's that human nature don't change. Whether you're hustling on the streets of Chicago or navigating the digital highways, the same rules apply. People can be sweet-talked, and they can be threatened. And when you combine the two? Well, that's when the magic happens.

Back in my day, if you wanted to run a racket, you needed a crew, a territory, and some real guts. Today? All you need is a computer, an internet connection, and some know-how. But the principles? They're the same. It's all about power, control, and making a quick buck. So, whether you're navigating the dark alleys of Chicago or the dark web, always remember: trust no one, keep your friends close and your enemies closer, and always, always have a backup plan. Because in this game, it's adapt or get left behind. And ol' Vinnie "the Squid" Marconi... He ain't getting left behind.

So, next time you're thinking about cybersecurity, remember ol' Vinnie's advice. Protect yourself against those smooth talkers, and always be on the lookout for the hidden "gun." Because in this game, it's always better to be one step ahead.

Chapter 2: Don't Keep all your Eggs in One Basket

Listen up, kid, 'cause I'm only gonna say this once. In our line of work, back in the dirty thirties, we knew the score. Never, and I mean never, put all your eggs in one basket. You wanna stay ahead of the Feds and outsmart the other gangs? You gotta play it smart, spread your loot, and keep your business diversified. Ain't no point in makin' it easy for the coppers or the competition to take you down.

See, back in the day, we didn't survive on muscle alone. Nah, the real brains knew how to spread the risk. One stash here, another there, a couple of fronts to keep the heat off, and a network of wise guys who knew how to keep their mouths shut. You didn't survive long by being a sitting duck, see? You kept your cards close to your chest and never let anyone know where the real jackpot was stashed.

Now, you think the cyber crooks today are any different? Ha! They may be hiding behind screens instead of fedoras, but the game ain't changed. Concentrate all your dough or your secrets in one spot, and you're just askin' for some hacker to come along and clean you out. The smart play is to spread it around, back it up, and make sure that no two-bit hacker can knock you out with one lucky punch.

This chapter, we're gonna break it down for ya, old-school style. We're talkin' the kind of street smarts that kept us outta the clink and how you can use the same tricks to keep your digital operation tight. So, sit back, pay attention, and learn from the best. 'Cause in this game, the stakes are high, and only the wise guys come out on top.

Here are some ways this we tried to keep our eggs safe, if ya get my drift:

- **Diversifying Revenue Streams:** We often engaged in various illegal activities such as bootlegging, gambling, extortion, and prostitution. Relying on multiple sources of income meant that if one operation was shut down or compromised by the boys in blue, others could continue to generate revenue.

- **Multiple Safehouses:** To avoid capture, my buddies would use multiple safehouses. Relying on a single hideout increased the risk of being caught. By having several locations, they could move around and evade coppers more effectively.

- **Spread of Power and Control:** Dons and capos would delegate responsibilities to trusted associates and soldiers to spread out their operations. Concentrating all power and activities in one place made it easier for our rivals or Feds to dismantle their operations.

- **Money Laundering:** My associates would launder money through various businesses and financial institutions to avoid detection. Using a single method or institution could lead to easy tracing and confiscation of their assets by the coppers.

Here's how you might try applying this idea of "diversification" in the modern world of cyber security and Internet safety:

- **Data Segmentation and Redundancy:** Look, you don't put all your dough in one joint, right? Same goes for your data.

Spread it out over different spots, and make sure you got backups. If one place gets hit, you ain't gonna lose the whole stash.

How do ya like these eggs? (Midjourney, 2024)

- **Multi-Factor Authentication (MFA):** Trustin' just one password? That's like walkin' into a speakeasy without a back-up piece. You need more than just one layer of protection. Make the goons try a few different tricks before they get through. It's like havin' a couple of tough guys at the door, not just one.

- **Diverse Security Protocols:** You wouldn't just carry a pistol when you might need a Tommy gun, would ya? Same goes for your security. Mix it up with firewalls, encryption, and keep an eye on things regularly. Don't put all your trust in just one method, or you'll end up in a pine box.

- **Backups and Disaster Recovery:** Always have a plan B, capisce? Regular backups and a solid recovery plan mean if something goes sideways, you can get back on your feet quick. Don't be that sap who loses it all because he didn't think ahead.

- **Vendor and Supply Chain Management:** You don't rely on just one guy to move your goods, do ya? Same thing here. Spread your risks by using different vendors and always keep an eye on 'em. If one of 'em slips up, you gonna be left holdin' the bag.

- **Decentralized Network Architecture:** Keep your operations spread out, just like how you'd never keep all your bootlegging in one warehouse. If one part of the network gets hit, the whole operation doesn't come crashing down. It's about keepin' things flexible and tough to crack.

That's how you keep things tight and make sure no one pulls a fast one on ya. Keep your eyes open, spread your risks, and always have a backup plan. Here are few examples where my associates could have done better at keeping their eggs safe.

1. Meyer Lansky and the Cuban Casino Empire
Alright, kid, let me paint you a picture. It's the 1950s, and Meyer Lansky, one of the sharpest minds in the underworld, sees an opportunity that's too good to pass up. The guy's already made a name for himself back in the States, with his fingers in everything from gambling joints to loan sharking. But Lansky's always thinking bigger, always looking for the next big score. And then he spots it: Cuba. Just a stone's throw from Florida, but far enough from Uncle Sam's reach. Cuba was a paradise for gamblers, tourists, and anyone

looking for a good time. And it was a place where Lansky could build something big, something untouchable... or so he thought.

Lansky cozies up to Fulgencio Batista, the Cuban dictator at the time, and the two strike a deal. Batista's government was as crooked as they come, and Lansky knew how to work that angle. He starts pouring money into Havana, turning it into a gambling mecca. We're talking high-end casinos, luxurious hotels, nightclubs with top-tier entertainers, the whole works. Lansky wasn't just building a few joints; he was turning Havana into the Las Vegas of the Caribbean. By the mid-50s, Lansky's Cuban operations were raking in millions. The tourists were flocking to Havana, the money was rolling in, and Lansky was sitting pretty, thinking he had the world by the tail. (Deitche, 2019)

Consequence: But here's where the story takes a turn. Lansky, for all his smarts, got too comfortable, too confident in his Cuban empire. He bet everything on Havana, put most of his resources and focus on the island. And then, in 1959, the whole game changed. Fidel Castro's revolution wasn't just another political shuffle. This was a full-blown takeover. Castro and his revolutionaries weren't interested in playing ball with the likes of Lansky. They wanted to kick out all the foreign influences, especially the American mobsters who were running the show.

In no time, Castro's government nationalized everything. They took control of the casinos, the hotels, the whole shebang. They smashed slot machines, closed down the gambling dens, and chased Lansky and his crew right out of Havana. Overnight, Lansky's golden goose was cooked. He lost millions ,some say upwards of $7 million, which back then was a fortune and more importantly, he lost the steady stream of cash that had been fueling his other operations. It was a devastating blow, the kind that could knock even a guy like Lansky off his game. All those years of work, all that money invested, and it was gone in a heartbeat.

Now, this is where the old saying comes in, "Don't keep all your eggs in one basket." Lansky, for all his brilliance, forgot this golden rule. He put all his faith, all his money, into one big play. Cuba was his basket, and when Castro tipped it over, Lansky lost everything in it. But imagine if Lansky had played it a little different. Instead of going all-in on Cuba, what if he had spread his investments around?

Say he'd put some money into casinos in South America, where the governments were more stable, or diversified into legitimate businesses back in the States. Maybe even expanded his operations in Las Vegas, which was just starting to boom. If he'd done that, when Cuba went south, Lansky would've still had revenue coming in from other places. Sure, losing Havana would've hurt, but it wouldn't have been the knockout punch that it was.

And it's not just about geography, either. Lansky could've diversified the types of businesses he was into. Instead of just focusing on gambling, he could've put some of that cash into real estate, entertainment, or even legitimate businesses that wouldn't crumble with a change in government. By having his hands in different pies, Lansky would've had a safety net, something to fall back on when the Cuban empire collapsed.

The point is, in our line of work, or any line of work, really, you can't afford to bet everything on one roll of the dice. You gotta spread your risks, make sure that if one deal goes belly up, you've got others that'll keep you afloat. Lansky's mistake was thinking that Cuba was a sure thing, and in this world, there's no such thing as a sure thing.

Lessons Learned:

- **Don't Become Overconfident:** Lansky was too confident in the stability of his Cuban empire. He believed that his close relationship with Batista's corrupt government made his operations untouchable.
  Lesson: Overconfidence can blind you to potential risks.

Always consider worst-case scenarios and prepare for unexpected changes.

- **Have a Backup Plan:** Lansky had no fallback plan when Cuba's political situation changed, which resulted in him losing millions and a key revenue stream.
  Lesson: Always have a backup plan. If one venture fails, you need alternative sources of income or options to recover.

- **Long-Term Thinking Is Key:**
  Lansky was focused on the immediate profits and glamour of Havana but didn't plan for the long term.
  Lesson: Successful ventures require long-term thinking and contingency planning. Be ready to pivot if things go south, and consider how changes in the future might impact your business.

Cybersecurity Relevance: Ah, Lansky, the brainy one. The guy builds his empire in Cuba, thinks he's untouchable 'cause he's got friends in high places. But what happens when the tides turn? Castro comes in and, boom, Lansky's investments are gone, just like that. In cybersecurity, putting all your bets on one system or one security measure? That's like Lansky betting everything on Havana. You gotta spread your risks, see? Make sure you're not depending on one firewall or one vendor, 'cause when that goes down, you're left with nothin'. Diversify, kid, or you'll end up just like ol' Meyer—outta business overnight.

So, take a lesson from Lansky's fall from grace. Whether you're running a criminal empire or just trying to make a buck, always have a backup plan. Diversify your investments, spread out your risks, and never, ever put all your eggs in one basket. That's how you survive in this game, and that's how you stay on top, no matter what comes your way.

2. **The Fall of the Kansas City Crime Family**

Alright, listen close, 'cause this one's got a lesson you don't wanna forget. Back in the 1970s and 1980s, the Kansas City crime family was runnin' hot under the leadership of Nick Civella. This guy was no slouch. He knew the streets, knew how to make a buck, and knew how to keep the coppers at bay. But like any smart operator, he was always lookin' for that one big score. And boy, did he find it in Las Vegas. The Kansas City mob got deep into the action in Sin City, but they weren't just hittin' the tables; they were skimming profits off the top of the biggest casinos on the Strip. Civella and his crew were pullin' in millions, makin' money before the casinos even knew it was missin'. It was like takin' candy from a baby, and for a while, it seemed like the perfect setup.

Consequence: But here's where things went sideways. See, the Kansas City mob got too comfortable with that Vegas dough. They were makin' so much easy money, they started thinkin' they were untouchable. But when you're rakin' in that kind of cash, the Feds are bound to take notice. And that's exactly what happened. The G-Men launched Operation Strawman in the late '70s, a full-blown investigation aimed right at the heart of the mob's skimming operation. They tapped phones, turned informants, and slowly started pullin' the whole thing apart.

By the time they were done, the jig was up. The Feds nailed Civella and his top guys to the wall. Convictions started comin' down like rain, and the Kansas City family's golden goose was cooked. With the Vegas skimming operation blown up, the mob was left high and dry. Their main source of income had gone up in smoke, and without that cash flow, the whole family started to crumble. They were so focused on milkin' Vegas that they didn't have nothin' else to fall back on when it all went to hell. (Ouseley, 2010)

Now, if Civella had taken a page outta the old playbook and remembered the rule, "Don't keep all your eggs in one basket," maybe things would've turned out different. But he got greedy, see? He put all his chips on one hand, thinkin' that Vegas money would keep flowin' forever. But when the Feds busted up that racket, he was left with nothin' but a lotta hot air and empty pockets.

If Civella had hedged his bets, the Kansas City mob wouldn't have been so easy to take down. Imagine if they'd diversified, gotten into different rackets, or even expanded their operations into other cities. Maybe they could've invested in clubs, booze, or gotten into real estate scams, where the Feds would've had a tougher time pinning 'em down. Hell, even if they'd put some of that dirty money into legitimate businesses, they would've had somethin' to keep 'em afloat when the hammer came down in Vegas.

Civella should've known better. You don't put all your trust in one score, no matter how sweet it looks. The smart move would've been to spread out, keep the cash flowin' from a dozen different places. That way, when the Feds shut down one operation, you still got others bringin' in the dough. But Civella and his boys got too comfortable, too lazy, and it cost 'em everything. They learned the hard way that when you put all your eggs in one basket, you're just askin' for someone to come along and smash 'em.

Lessons Learned:

- **Overconfidence in One Revenue Stream**: The Kansas City mob was making millions from skimming Las Vegas casinos, but they became too dependent on this single source of income. Their confidence in the Vegas operation led them to believe it was untouchable.
  Lesson: Overconfidence in a single operation makes you vulnerable if it falls apart.

- **Failure to Diversify**: The Kansas City mob focused almost exclusively on their Vegas operations, failing to branch out into other rackets or cities. When the Vegas cash cow dried up, they had nothing else to rely on.
  Lesson: Always diversify. By having multiple streams of

income or areas of focus, a setback in one area won't cripple the entire operation.

- **Lack of Backup Plan**: Civella and his crew were so focused on the easy money from Vegas that they didn't have a backup plan for when it fell apart. Without alternative income sources, the family began to crumble.
  Lesson: Always have a contingency plan. In business or life, it's critical to plan for potential setbacks and ensure there's something else to fall back on when things go wrong.

What da ya say to a buck a hole? (Midjourney, 2023)

- **The Importance of Spreading Risk**:
  If Civella had spread the Kansas City mob's operations into

other rackets or legitimate businesses, they might have survived the Vegas bust. Diversifying into different industries or cities would have made it harder for the Feds to target their entire operation.

Lesson: Spread your risk across multiple ventures, industries, or regions. This way, if one part of the operation goes down, you still have others to rely on.

Cybersecurity Relevance: Civella's crew thought they were set, rakin' in the cash from Vegas. Too bad they were leanin' on just one operation. The moment the Feds figured out the skim, the whole thing crumbled. That's a lesson in cybersecurity: you rely too much on one security system, one strategy, you're askin' for trouble. Hackers find that weak spot, and you're outta luck. Spread your defenses, don't put all your eggs in one basket, capisce?

Don't ever get too comfortable. Diversify your operations, spread your risks, and make sure you've got a backup plan for when the hammer comes down. The Kansas City mob fell because they didn't follow this simple rule, and they paid the price. Don't make the same mistake. In this game, you gotta be smart, you gotta be careful, and you gotta always have one foot out the door, ready to move when the heat's on. That's how you stay in business, and that's how you stay alive.

3. The Rise and Fall of Frank Costello

Let me tell ya about Frank Costello, one of the sharpest minds ever to run the streets. They called him the "Prime Minister of the Underworld," and for good reason. Costello wasn't just some two-bit hood. He was the guy who had everyone, from politicians to judges, in his pocket. The man practically owned the city, all because of one thing: gambling. Costello built himself a golden empire on illegal gambling operations. Slots, bookies, casinos, you name it, he had a piece of it. And it wasn't just in New York, either; he had his fingers in gambling joints all across the country. He was rakin' in millions, and with that kind of dough, he had the muscle to back it up. Costello was sittin' on top of the world, untouchable... or so he thought.

But here's the rub. Costello put almost all his energy into gambling. Now, don't get me wrong, it was makin' him a fortune, but it was also makin' him a target. You gotta remember, when you're makin' that much noise, someone's gonna start lookin' your way. And in Costello's case, that someone was Vito Genovese. Genovese was another big shot, but he was hungrier, meaner, and jealous of Costello's power. He didn't like how much control Costello had, and he figured the quickest way to the top was by knockin' Costello off his throne.

Consequence: So, in 1957, Vito made his move. He sends a trigger man to take out Costello, and it was close...real close. The hitman squeezes the trigger, the bullet grazes Costello's head, but the old fox survives. Now, any other guy might've gone to war, but Costello was no fool. He knew the score. He was gettin' older, and the streets were changin'. Instead of fightin' it out, Costello decides to retire. He steps down from the mafia life, handin' over his empire, his power, everything.

Now here's the thing, when Costello stepped down, he didn't just lose control of his gambling operations. He lost his protection, his influence, his clout. See, his whole empire was built on one foundation: gambling. And once he gave that up, he didn't have nothin' else to fall back on. Genovese took over, and Costello, the guy who used to be king, was left with nothin' but his life and that was only because he bowed out gracefully. (Serena, 2024)

Here's where Costello went wrong, and it's a mistake you don't wanna make. He put all his eggs in one basket, gambling. Sure, it made him rich, but it also painted a big target on his back. When Vito decided to make his move, it was easy for him to know where to hit. Costello didn't have a diversified operation, didn't have other streams of income to keep him afloat when the heat came down.

Now, if Costello had been a little smarter about it, he could've spread his interests around. Think about it. What if he'd gotten into other rackets? Maybe drugs, like some of the other families were startin' to do, or maybe real estate, which was always a safe bet. Hell, he could've put some of that gambling money into legitimate businesses, used it to launder his cash and give himself a legitimate front. With a diversified empire, he would've had more protection, more ways to keep his enemies off balance. When the hit came, if it even came at all, Costello could've stepped back from gambling without losin' his entire operation.

Costello was too focused, too set on one way of makin' money. And that's where the old saying comes in "Don't keep all your eggs in one basket." In this life, or any life, you gotta spread the risk. Diversify your operations, keep your enemies guessin', and always have a way out if things go south. Costello was a smart guy, but he forgot that even the smartest can fall if they don't cover all their bases.
So here's the takeaway, kid: Don't ever put all your trust in one thing, no matter how good it seems. Diversify, keep your hands in a few different pies, and never let anyone know exactly where your money's comin' from. That way, if someone tries to take you down, they're gonna have a hell of a time doin' it. Costello learned that the hard way, and it cost him his empire. Don't make the same mistake. Keep your options open, spread out your interests, and you'll stay one step ahead of the game. That's how you survive, and that's how you stay on top.

Lessons Learned:

- **Failure to Evolve with Changing Times:** As the streets and the mafia world evolved, Costello did not adapt, which ultimately led to his downfall. He didn't diversify his operations or adapt to new opportunities, such as drugs or real estate, which other families were starting to explore.
  Lesson: Always evolve and adapt to changing circumstances.

Diversify into new areas when opportunities arise, and stay ahead of your competitors.

- **Retreat Without a Backup Plan:** When Costello decided to retire after the assassination attempt, he gave up everything. He lost his control over the gambling racket, his protection, and his influence, leaving him vulnerable and powerless. **Lesson:** Always have a backup plan before stepping down from a key position of power. Ensure you still have influence or other sources of strength when you transition out of a dominant role.

- **Power Comes From Diversification:** Costello's power was concentrated in gambling, which made it easy for his enemies to know where to strike. If he had spread his interests into other rackets, he could have maintained control and kept his enemies guessing. **Lesson:** Diversification in operations helps you stay ahead of your rivals and makes it harder for them to dismantle your empire.

Cybersecurity Relevance: Frank was a smart operator, but he had one fatal flaw—he put all his chips on the gambling racket. When Vito came for him, Costello had nowhere else to go, no other angles. Same goes for your cyber defenses, pal. If you focus all your resources on one type of security, the moment someone finds a way around it, you're finished. Diversify your strategies. Make it hard for 'em to take you down. Costello didn't, and look where it got him.

For all you's that think the big companies and security gurus have this diversity thing figured out, guess again. Here are a few examples were spreading out some eggs could'a gone a long way.

4. The CrowdStrike Outage in 2024 and McAfee Outage in 2010

Alright, kid, it's 2024, and CrowdStrike, the big shot in the cyber world for endpoint protection, pushes out an updated to all their customers. But things don't go a planned, those PCs that got the update are now crippled with a Blue Screen of Death (BSOD) when they start-up. This resulted in the largest IT outage in history. (Beaty, 2024)

Now if you'd never met the BSOD it was probably a surprise, but for those in the know it was downright devastating. Especially when it was on their very important company servers. The BSOD is Microsoft's way of telling you that this machine is dead and without help it will stay that way.

Turns out the update CrowdStrike sent out was not ready for prime-time and had one file in it that caused these BSODs. The CrowdStrike Quality Assurance (QA) team missed this and the updated was sent out globally to all users.

Strangely enough something very similar happened back in 2010 with McAfee. McAfee at the time, just like CrowdStrike in 2024, was a big shot in the endpoint protection racket. McAfee sent out an update know as a "DAT" file to their users world-wide and caused a global shut-down of PCs running Windows XP. Even more interesting is that McAfee's CTO when this happens becomes the co-founder of and is the CEO of CrowdStrike in 2024. (Pandey, 2024)

In the hours following the initial panic of CrowdStrike causing millions of computers world-wide to stop working, CrowdStrike informed the world they could recover their devices by removing an offending file and re-booting their machines. Sounds easy right, not really when you are talking about having to manually safe boot each machine, remove the file, and reboot (Bott, n.d.). This process required an engineer to reach out and touch each and every devices, none of those magical automations tools would help in this case.

Consequence: This wasn't just a minor inconvenience; it was a full-blown disaster for a lot of companies. Companies that were banking on CrowdStrike to keep their systems locked up tight were suddenly shutdown.

The CrowdStrike outage is estimated to have impacted 25% of Fortune 500 companies and cost them approximately $5.4 billion. (darkreading.com, 2024)

The outage caused more than 7,000 flights to be delayed or canceled over several days. Ports from New York to Los Angeles and Rotterdam reported temporary shutdowns, and air freight hubs were also impacted, with thousands of flights being delayed or grounded. Besides airlines, other impacted industries included healthcare, finance, manufacturing, and retail. For example, hospitals and clinics were unable to access patient records and communications, while banks and financial services were prevented from data management and transactions.

Now, here's where that old saying, "Don't keep all your eggs in one basket," hits like a two-by-four to the noggin. CrowdStrike, for all their smarts, made the same mistake McAfee did before them. Companies that only used CrowdStrike for some of their enterprise but not all of it, were back online much faster that those that were 100% dependent on CrowdStrike.

If everyone had played it smarter, they would've spread their operation across a few different endpoint protection outfits. You know, mix it up a bit. That way, if one goes belly up, the others keep the lights on, and nobody's left in the dark.

But no, most companies stuck to one provider and put all their eggs in one basket. Diversification isn't just for the Wall Street types; it's how you stay alive in any racket, digital or otherwise. And the same goes for the businesses that got burned by CrowdStrike's outage. When you put all your trust in one vendor, thinkin' you'r safe, and that vendor slips, you take the fall too.

Lessons Learned:

- **Overreliance on a Single Provider:** Companies that depended entirely on CrowdStrike for endpoint protection were the most severely impacted by the outage. Those that had diversified their security solutions were able to recover faster. **Lesson:** Don't rely solely on one provider or service. Always diversify your vendors to mitigate risks in case one fails.

- **Thorough Quality Assurance is Crucial:** The entire issue stemmed from a missed problem during CrowdStrike's quality assurance testing. One faulty file led to global outages, similar to McAfee's error years before.
  Lesson: Invest heavily in quality assurance and testing, especially when deploying mission-critical updates. One small mistake can lead to catastrophic results.

- **Backup Plans and Fail-Safes are Essential:** Companies that had a backup or alternative endpoint protection provider recovered much faster. Those fully dependent on CrowdStrike were left scrambling with no immediate recovery options.
  Lesson: Always have a backup plan. In technology, as in business, things can go wrong quickly. Having redundancies and alternative solutions helps mitigate the impact of unexpected failures.

- **Diversification as a Protective Strategy:** Companies that didn't put all their eggs in the CrowdStrike basket were able to weather the storm much better. Diversification of vendors, systems, and solutions allowed for quicker recovery.
  Lesson: Diversify your vendors, tools, and solutions. In cybersecurity, as in any industry, depending on one solution

can lead to disaster. Spreading risk across multiple providers creates resilience.

Cybersecurity Relevance: Now this here's a prime example of what happens when you rely too much on one big shot. CrowdStrike was supposed to be the top dog, protectin' everyone's systems, but when their update messed up, it was lights out. Thousands of businesses took a hit 'cause they didn't have a backup. Same thing happened with McAfee back in the day. The lesson? Don't put all your trust in one provider, kid. You need a fallback, a plan B, so when things go sideways, you're not caught with your pants down.

So, here's the deal, kid: whether you're pushin' or getting updates, runnin' a business, or just tryin' to keep your systems safe, you can't afford to put all your trust in one thing. Spread your risks, have backups, and always have a way out if things go south. That's how you stay in the game, and that's how you avoid gettin' taken down by a single mistake. It's the kinda lesson that can save your skin.

5. Sony PlayStation Network Hack (2011)

Back in 2011, when Sony, yeah, the big cheese in the entertainment racket, got itself in one helluva jam. We're talkin' about the PlayStation Network, or PSN as the gamers like to call it. This thing was Sony's crown jewel, the heart and soul of the online gaming world. Millions of players from all over the globe were hooked up to this network, playin' games, buyin' stuff, and chattin' with their buddies. But Sony made a mistake, and it was a big one.

Here's what went down. Some wiseguys in the cyber world decided to make a move on Sony. They cracked into the PlayStation Network, and what did they find? A motherlode, personal information on 77 million users, just sittin' there, ripe for the takin'. Names, addresses, emails, and even some credit card details. It was all there, like a stack of cash in an unguarded safe. Sony had all their user data centralized, all in one spot, thinkin' they were untouchable. But the moment those hackers got in, they cleaned the place out.

Who brought Cheetos and Mountain Dew?

Consequence: The fallout? Oh, it was bad, real bad. Sony had to pull the plug on the PlayStation Network for 24 days. That's right, nearly a month of gamers left in the dark, unable to play their games, buy new ones, or even talk to their pals. You can imagine the uproar. But it wasn't just about the gamers bein' ticked off. The real damage was the personal info that got swiped. Sony's customers were left worryin' about identity theft, fraud, and who knows what else. The government started breathin' down Sony's neck, lookin' into how they let this happen. And Sony's reputation? Took a dive like a two-bit crook caught red-handed. (Sinclair, 2021)

Financially, Sony got whacked. We're talkin' an estimated $171 million in immediate costs, cleanup, compensation, legal fees, the whole shebang. But the real pain was in the trust they lost. People started wonderin' if Sony could really protect their information. Future sales? They took a hit too. Once you lose trust, it's a long road to get it back.

Let's talk about where Sony went wrong, and how, "Don't keep all your eggs in one basket," coulda saved their skins. See, Sony made the rookie mistake of centralizin' all their data and security in one place. It was like stackin' all your cash in one safe and thinkin' nobody would ever crack it. But when those cyber crooks got in, they hit the jackpot. If Sony had spread out that data and decentralized it across multiple systems. They coulda made it a whole lot harder for those hackers to get everything in one go.

Imagine if Sony had set things up so that different pieces of data were stored in different places, each with its own security. The hackers mighta broken into one system, sure, but they wouldn't have gotten their hands on the whole enchilada. They woulda had to work a lot harder, and by then, Sony mighta caught on and shut 'em down before they could do any real damage.

And another thing, Sony coulda beefed up their defenses with multi-factor authentication (MFA). What they had was like lockin' the door with a rusty old padlock. MFA woulda been like addin' a few more locks, a guard dog, and maybe even a guy with a shotgun sittin' out front. If Sony had made it so you needed more than just a password to get in, like a code sent to your phone, or even a fingerprint, the hackers woulda had a much tougher time gettin' what they wanted. Even if they cracked one layer, they'd still have more to get through. So, what's the lesson here, kid? Simple. Whether it's your money, your data, or your trust, you gotta spread it out. Diversify your defenses, have backup plans, and make sure that if one thing goes down, the whole operation doesn't go with it. Sony learned that the hard way, but you don't have to.

Lessons Learned:

- **Don't Centralize Sensitive Data:**
  Sony made the critical error of storing all personal information for 77 million users in one central system. Once the hackers got in, they accessed everything in one hit.
  Lesson: Avoid centralizing all sensitive data in one place. Decentralizing data storage across multiple systems makes it harder for attackers to access everything in one breach.

- **The Importance of Redundancy and Backups:** Sony failed to have an effective backup plan to prevent or mitigate the damage of the breach. Decentralized security and data storage could have slowed down or even stopped the hackers from getting away with all the data.
  Lesson: Always have redundant security measures and decentralized data storage to reduce the risk of losing everything in one attack. Spread your risk across multiple systems to minimize damage.

- **The Role of Multi-Factor Authentication (MFA):**
  Sony's lack of MFA made it easy for hackers to gain access. Adding MFA would have required the hackers to bypass additional layers of security, making it much harder to breach the system.
  Lesson: Implementing MFA and additional security layers makes it significantly harder for hackers to gain access. Even if they crack one layer, they still have more to overcome.

Cybersecurity Relevance: Sony thought they had it all locked up, millions of users playin' on their network. But when the hackers got in, they cleaned Sony out, takin' user data like it was cash outta an open safe. Sony's mistake? They kept all their data in one place, thinkin' it was untouchable. That's a rookie move in cybersecurity. Always spread out your data, have layers of protection, or else you're beggin' for a digital stick-up.

6. OPM Data Breach (2015)

Let me twist your ear about a real mess that went down in 2015. A fiasco that even the wiseguys on the street would've seen comin' a mile away. We're talkin' about the Office of Personnel Management, or OPM for short. These mugs were supposed to be the gatekeepers for all the personal info of Uncle Sam's crew the government employees, from the pencil pushers to the spooks workin' undercover. They had it all: Social Security numbers, addresses, job histories, even fingerprints. But here's where they screwed the pooch, they put all that info in one big pot, thinkin' it was safe. It's like stashin' all your cash under one mattress and trustin' nobody's gonna find it.

Well, wouldn't ya know it, some smart operators from across the ocean, likely workin' for another outfit, got wind of this treasure trove. They did a little diggin', found a weak spot in OPM's defenses, and before you could say "Jackie Robinson," they were in. And they didn't just take a peek. They grabbed the whole kit and caboodle. The personal data of 21.5 million folks, snatched up like candy from a baby. Background checks, fingerprints, all the juicy details gone. It was like hittin' the jackpot, and OPM never saw it comin'.

Consequence: The aftermath? Oh, it was a disaster of epic proportions. Imagine, the personal details of millions of government workers, includin' folks with access to some of the country's biggest secrets, now in the hands of who-knows-who. This wasn't just about identity theft—this was a national security nightmare. We're talkin' blackmail, espionage, the kind of stuff that could make a guy disappear. And OPM? They were caught with their pants down, no two ways about it.

Congress, the media, and pretty much everyone else gave 'em a good thrashin'. Turns out these guys were runnin' on outdated systems, with security practices that were about as tight as a sieve. It was a miracle this hadn't happened sooner. The cleanup? It cost a bundle. Millions of taxpayer dollars down the drain, tryin' to patch things up. But the real hit was to the government's credibility. People started wonderin' if Uncle Sam could really keep anything safe. It was a black eye that would take a long time to heal.

Here's where, "Don't keep all your eggs in one basket," woulda saved their bacon. OPM made the rookie mistake of throwin' all that sensitive info into one big ol' basket without so much as a decent lock on it. When the hackers got in, they cleaned the whole place out. But if OPM had been smart, they woulda spread that data around and distributed it across multiple systems, each one locked up tighter than a bank vault.

Let me paint you a picture. Instead of stackin' all that data in one place, OPM coulda split it up, puttin' different pieces in different systems, each with its own layer of protection. You get your Social Security numbers over here, your fingerprints over there, and everything wrapped up in some serious encryption. Even if those hackers had managed to crack one system, they wouldn't have gotten the whole haul. It woulda been like breakin' into a vault only to find a single safety deposit box, not the whole treasure. That's how you play the game when the stakes are this high.

And another thing, they shoulda been keepin' a much closer eye on their security. Regular checkups, audits, multi-factor authentication the works. If they'd had these measures in place, they mighta caught the punks in the act, or at least limited the damage. Instead, they were runnin' blind, and it cost 'em big time.

So, the lesson here is simple, don't put all your eggs in one basket, especially when it comes to the kinda info that could bring down the house. Spread it out, lock it up, and always be on the lookout for someone tryin' to pull a fast one. If OPM had done that, they mighta avoided one of the biggest security screw-ups in government history. Here you have it, kid. Whether you're runnin' the streets like we did back in the dirty thirties, or you're tryin' to keep your digital empire safe in today's world, the rules ain't changed much. The biggest mistake you can make is puttin' all your trust in one place, one score, or one plan. It's like hangin' a "kick me" sign on your back and waitin' for someone to take you out.

The wise guys who lasted the longest, whether they were runnin' numbers or lockin' down cyber networks, were the ones who knew how to spread their risks. They didn't put all their loot in one spot, didn't rely on just one hideout, and never trusted just one person with all the power. They knew the game could change in an instant, and when it did, they had a dozen different ways to stay ahead. Take a look at Lansky, Civella, and Costello, they were sharp, no doubt, but they got too comfortable, too confident, and they paid the price. The same goes for the tech giants today who didn't learn the lessons of the past. They got hit hard because they didn't spread out their eggs, didn't diversify their operations, and didn't have a solid backup plan.

Lessons Learned:

- **Outdated Security Practices are Dangerous**:
  OPM was using outdated systems with weak security measures, making it easier for hackers to exploit vulnerabilities.
  Lesson: Always keep security systems up to date. Cybersecurity threats evolve quickly, and using outdated technology leaves you exposed to attacks.

- **Spread Out Data to Limit Damage**:
  If OPM had spread data across multiple systems, with different layers of security, the hackers would not have been able to access everything so easily.

Lesson: Spread sensitive information across multiple systems and secure each one with strong, distinct protections. This ensures that even if one system is breached, attackers cannot access all the data.

- **Regular Security Audits and Monitoring are Essential**:
  OPM was running without regular security audits or sufficient monitoring, allowing the breach to go unnoticed until the damage was done.
  Lesson: Conduct regular security audits, and use real-time monitoring systems to detect and respond to threats before they escalate. Early detection can limit the scope of damage.

- **Multi-Factor Authentication (MFA) is Crucial**:
  OPM's weak security setup lacked multi-factor authentication, which could have slowed down or prevented the hackers from gaining access to the data.
  Lesson: Implement MFA to add an additional layer of protection. MFA can make it much harder for attackers to gain unauthorized access, even if they have login credentials.

Cybersecurity Relevance: The OPM breach was a hit so big, even the Feds got rattled. Hackers walked off with millions of sensitive records. Think of it like robbin' a vault full of secrets. In the world of cybersecurity, it's a stark reminder that even the big boys can get burned if they don't patch up vulnerabilities. Always be lookin' for weak spots, or you'll end up on the wrong side of a breach.

So, remember this, whether you're buildin' an empire on the streets or in the cyber world, you gotta keep your options open. Diversify, spread your risks, and always have a way out if things go south. It's the only way to stay on top and avoid gettin' knocked out by a single punch. In this game, it's the wise guys who survive, and the ones who keep all their eggs in one basket? They're the ones who end up on the wrong side of history.

Chapter 3: Everyone's Got a Plan Until They Get Punched in the Mouth

Heya, folks! It's me again, Vinnie "the Squid" Marconi, back with another tale from the digital streets. Now, I've been in my fair share of scrapes and tussles, and there's one thing I've learned: it's one thing to talk a big game, but it's a whole 'nother ball game when you're staring down the barrel of a Tommy gun or taking a right hook to the jaw. As the modern pugilist, Mike Tyson, once quipped, "Everyone's got a plan until they get punched in the mouth." And lemme tell ya, that sentiment rings true in the world of cybersecurity too.

You see, in the glitzy world of speakeasies and poker tables, we had our ways of dealing with threats. A beef with a rival gang? We'd settle it in the alleyways. A cheat at the card table? Well, let's just say they'd be learning a tough lesson. But in your digital age, the punches come from places you least expect, and they hit hard.

The Plan: Every organization out there wants to be the bee's knees when it comes to cybersecurity. They've got their fancy firewalls, their encrypted data, and their two-factor whatsits. The good ones spend the dough and hope they've got it all figured out.

The Punch: But then, outta nowhere, WHAM! A cyberattack blindsides 'em. Maybe it's a phishing scam that tricks the big boss into handing over the keys to the kingdom. Or perhaps it's a piece of ransomware that locks up all their precious data. Suddenly, all those plans, all those protocols, they go out the window. Panic sets in, mistakes are made, and before you know it, they're in a world of hurt.

Now, I ain't saying this to scare ya. I'm saying it 'cause it's the truth. Just like in the rough and tumble world of 1930s Chicago, you've gotta be prepared for anything. You've gotta be nimble, adaptable, and always on your toes.

So, what's a modern-day gangster to do in the face of such threats? Well, here's a bit of advice from ol' Vinnie:

- **Expect the Unexpected:** Always be on the lookout for that sucker punch. It might come from a rival, or it might come from some faceless hacker halfway across the world. Stay vigilant.

- **Train Like You Fight:** It's one thing to have a plan on paper, but it's another to put it into action. Regularly test your cybersecurity measures. Run drills, simulate attacks, and table-top exercises to see how your team responds.

- **Learn from Your Mistakes:** Took a hit? Dust yourself off and figure out what went wrong. Patch up those vulnerabilities and come back stronger.

- **Trust No One... Completely:** In the world of cybersecurity, even your closest allies could be your downfall. An unintentional click on a malicious link, a misplaced password – always have checks and balances in place. Watch out for those 3rd party vendors too.

Where'd that punch come from? (Midjourney, 2023)

- **Keep Your Ears to the Ground:** Stay informed. The world of cyber threats is ever evolving. What worked today might not work tomorrow. Always be learning, always be adapting.

There you have it, pal. In the digital age, just like in the streets of Chicago, you've gotta be ready for anything. And remember, it ain't about how hard you hit; it's about how hard you can get hit and keep moving forward.

See here, I got a couple o' examples for ya..

1. The SolarWinds Hack (2020)

The SolarWinds Hack of 2020, a cybersecurity calamity that'll be talked about for years to come. It's the epitome of the phrase "Everyone's got a plan until they get punched in the mouth." So, let's roll up our sleeves and dig into the nitty-gritty of this cautionary tale, shall we? (Oladimeji & Kerner, 2023)

The Plan: A Symphony of Security Protocols

SolarWinds, a titan in the IT industry, had a plan that was more like a symphony, each security measure playing its part in a harmonious defense against cyber threats. They had firewalls, intrusion detection systems, and multi-factor authentication. They even had a dedicated team of cybersecurity experts monitoring their network 24/7. Their software was trusted by governments and Fortune 500 companies alike. They were the maestros of network management.

The Illusion of Invincibility

In the gangster world, you might think you're the kingpin, untouchable, invincible even. But let me tell ya, kid, that's when you're most vulnerable. SolarWinds thought they were invincible, but they were blindsided. They had a plan, but it wasn't foolproof.

The Art of Being Prepared for the Unthinkable

You see, in the underworld, you always prepare for the unthinkable. You've got hidden stashes, secret exits, and allies in high places. SolarWinds had a plan, but they didn't account for the unthinkable—a state-sponsored cyberattack that would exploit their very core: a routine software update.

The Sucker Punch from Left Field

The punch came outta nowhere. Russian hackers, crafty as they come, inserted malicious code into a routine software update. This wasn't just a jab; it was a haymaker, a sucker punch that left SolarWinds and its clients reeling. The scale was unprecedented, affecting U.S. government agencies, including the Department of Homeland Security and the Treasury, as well as major corporations. (Temple-Raston, 2021)

Once the breach was discovered, it was pandemonium. SolarWinds had to act fast. They had to identify which systems were compromised, isolate them, and then begin the painstaking process of rebuilding their security infrastructure. Their clients had to do the same, each realizing that their well-laid plans were shattered.

Lessons Learned:

- **Expect the Unexpected**: SolarWinds had a tight operation, thought they had all the angles covered. But just like in the streets, it's the hit you don't see that puts you down. Those Russian hackers slipped in through a routine update.
  Lesson: In cybersecurity, don't get too comfortable. Even when things seem solid, you gotta be ready for the sucker punch. Always stay on your toes and expect the unexpected.

- **Rapid Response is Key**:
  When SolarWinds got hit, they had to scramble, patch things up fast, and figure out where they went wrong. If you're slow to react, you're done for.
  Lesson: In cybersecurity, when things go south, it's all about how fast you can act. The quicker you can isolate the problem, the better your chances of surviving the hit.

- **Never Stop Learning**: SolarWinds thought their defenses were up to snuff, but in the cyber world, things change fast. What worked yesterday might not cut it tomorrow.
  Lesson: You gotta keep learning in this game. Keep updating your tools, trainin' your crew, and adaptin' to new threats. If you ain't keepin' up, you're fallin' behind.

- **Third-Party Risk Management**: SolarWinds' breach didn't come from inside their house, but from the software they used. Relying on outside vendors can be a weak link if you don't keep a close eye.
  Lesson: When you're dealing with third-party vendors, you're inheriting their problems. Always vet 'em thoroughly, 'cause if they slip up, it's your operation on the line.

- **Transparency and Communication**: When the breach came out, SolarWinds had to be straight with their customers and partners. In a crisis, how you handle the fallout makes a big difference.
  Lesson: In cybersecurity, clear communication during a breach is just as important as plugging the hole. Keep everyone informed to manage the damage and regain trust.

- **Post-Mortem Analysis**: After the breach, SolarWinds had to sit down and figure out exactly where things went wrong. You don't learn from mistakes unless you dig deep and analyze.
  Lesson: When the dust settles, always do a post-mortem. Look at what failed, what worked, and how to prevent it next time. That's how you keep getting better.

Cybersecurity Relevance: Ah, SolarWinds, that was a sucker punch if I ever saw one. The Russians slipped malware into a software update, hittin' targets like government agencies and big corporations all at once. It's like takin' over a speakeasy and using it to poison the whole city. You think your system's solid, then BAM! They're inside. What you gotta learn here, pal, is that even your best defenses can be turned against you if you're not watching every angle. In cybersecurity, trust ain't enough...you gotta verify, and verify again, capisce?

2. **The Colonial Pipeline Ransomware Attack (2021)**

The Colonial Pipeline Ransomware Attack of 2021, a tale that'll make you rethink the way you look at gas stations and pipelines. It's a story that perfectly embodies the phrase "Everyone's got a plan until they get punched in the mouth." So, let's fuel up and dive into this high-octane saga, shall we?

Hacker from back in my day. (Midjourney, 2023)

The Plan: A Pipeline of Security Measures

Colonial Pipeline, the big kahuna of fuel pipelines in the U.S., had a plan as sturdy as steel. They had firewalls, intrusion detection systems, and even a dedicated cybersecurity team. They were responsible for delivering the liquid gold—gasoline, diesel, and jet fuel—to a large chunk of the U.S. East Coast. They were a critical artery in the nation's energy infrastructure, and they knew it.

The Gangster Wisdom: Even Fortresses Can Be Breached

In the gangster world, you might have a secret hideout, complete with guards and a vault, but let me tell ya, even fortresses can be breached. Colonial Pipeline thought they were secure, but they didn't account for the cunning of their adversaries.

The Art of Being Prepared for All Scenarios

You see, in the underworld, you prepare for everything—from police raids to rival gang attacks. Colonial Pipeline had cybersecurity measures, but they weren't prepared for a ransomware attack of this magnitude.

The Knockout Punch from DarkSide

The punch came from a group called DarkSide, and boy, did it land hard. Using ransomware, they forced Colonial Pipeline to shut down its operations. This wasn't just a digital catastrophe; it had real-world consequences. Gas stations ran dry, prices soared, and panic spread like wildfire. (Javers, 2021)

The Art of Crisis Management: From Digital to Physical

Once the attack was confirmed, Colonial Pipeline had to act swiftly. They had to shut down the pipeline to contain the breach, coordinate with law enforcement, and negotiate with the attackers. They also had to manage a public relations crisis as the nation watched gas prices skyrocket and stations run dry.

Lessons Learned:

- **Prepare for the Worst**: Colonial Pipeline thought they had a solid setup, firewalls, intrusion detection, the works. But DarkSide hit 'em where it hurt, bringing the whole operation to a standstill.
  Lesson: In cybersecurity, don't just think you're safe. Always prepare for the worst. The big hit will come when you least expect it.

- **Rapid Response and Adaptability**: When DarkSide hit, Colonial Pipeline had to move fast, shift from defense to damage control, and manage the fallout.
  Lesson: When you're under attack, it's all about how fast you can respond. Adapt on the fly, or you'll be left picking up the pieces.

- **Public Communication**: The breach had folks panicking, gas stations running dry, and prices spiking. Colonial had to manage not just the breach, but the public's freak-out.
  Lesson: In a crisis, how you talk to the public can make or break you. Keep 'em informed, or they'll turn on ya fast.

- **Third-Party Assessments**: After the smoke cleared, it was obvious that Colonial could've benefited from outside eyes looking over their systems.
  Lesson: Get third-party assessments to find the cracks in your defenses before someone else does. Fresh eyes can see what you might miss.

- **Government Coordination**: With the whole East Coast hurting for fuel, Colonial had to team up with government agencies for support and investigation.
  Lesson: When the stakes are high, workin' with the government ain't just an option. It's a necessity. Make sure you're coordinated with the right folks when things go south.

- **Holistic Security**: The pipeline shutting down didn't just mess up data. It messed up the entire fuel supply chain. This wasn't just a computer problem. It was an infrastructure disaster. **Lesson**: Cybersecurity ain't just about protecting files. It's about protecting the whole operation. One weak link, and the whole system can collapse.

Cybersecurity Relevance: The Colonial Pipeline job? That was a real masterpiece, but not for the good guys. These hackers locked up the system like a vault, cutting off fuel to the whole East Coast. That's not just a digital problem, that's real-world chaos. It's like shuttin' down all the speakeasies at once, and watchin' the streets go dry. The lesson? In cybersecurity, your systems ain't just protecting your data, they're holdin' your whole operation together. One crack, and the whole pipeline goes dry.

So, whether you're a cybersecurity guru or a gangster, the lesson is clear: "Everyone's got a plan until they get punched in the mouth."

Here's a couple more for ya, kid.

3. The Lufthansa Heist (1978)

Ah, let's dive into a classic from the annals of mob history, shall we? The Lufthansa Heist of '78, a master plan orchestrated by the Lucchese crime family, is a tale that perfectly captures the essence of having a plan and then facing the unexpected punches.

The Plan: A Blueprint for the Perfect Heist

Jimmy Burke, an associate of the Lucchese crime family, had a plan that was as detailed as a blueprint. He got a tip from an inside man at the Lufthansa cargo building at JFK Airport. The tip was golden— literally. A vault filled with millions in untraceable cash and jewelry. The mobsters planned every detail, from disabling the alarm system to the getaway cars. They even had a plan for dividing the loot.

The Devil's in the Details

In the gangster world, planning a heist is like setting up dominoes. One wrong move, and the whole thing comes crashing down. Jimmy Burke and his crew thought of everything... or so they believed. They had a plan, but as we all know, even the best-laid plans can go awry.

The Art of Being Prepared for the Unforeseen

You see, in the underworld, you've got to prepare for the unforeseen. You might have a plan for the heist, but what about the aftermath? What's your plan for keeping everyone quiet, for laundering the money, for dealing with the heat that'll inevitably come down?

The Punch: The Fallout, The Real Heist

The punch came after the heist, and it was a doozy. The heist itself was a masterpiece, netting them around $5 million in cash and nearly a million in jewelry. But then came the fallout. Paranoia set in like a fog. The mobsters started worrying about snitches, about loose ends. And what did they do? They started eliminating their own, one by one. The real punch was the self-destruction that followed the heist. (Roman, 2023)

The Art of Managing Paranoia and Greed

Once the heist was successful, the real challenge began... managing the paranoia and greed that follows such a large score. Jimmy Burke found himself not just dividing loot but also deciding who could be trusted to keep quiet. The aftermath became a deadly game of trust and betrayal.

Lessons Learned:

- **Plan for the Aftermath**: Jimmy Burke and his crew pulled off the heist of the century, but they forgot to plan for what came next, the paranoia, the loose ends, the heat.
  Lesson: A successful job ain't just about grabbin' the loot, it's about what happens after. Whether it's a heist or a cyber job, you gotta plan for the fallout or you'll be running scared.

- **Trust, but Verify**: Burke trusted his crew, but trust in the underworld ain't worth much without verification. Snitches and weak links can sink a whole operation.
  Lesson: In cybersecurity or crime, trust is earned, but always verified. Make sure the folks you're countin' on won't flip when things get hot.

- **Greed is a Double-Edged Sword**: That $5 million score blinded 'em. Greed took over, and everyone wanted more. When you chase too much, you risk losing it all.
  Lesson: Big scores come with big risks. In both heists and cybersecurity, greed can make you careless. Keep a clear head or risk it all coming down on you.

- **The Bigger the Heist, the Bigger the Fallout**: Stealing millions draws attention. The bigger the job, the bigger the problems that follow. Jimmy Burke found that out the hard way.
  Lesson: The bigger the operation, the bigger the mess you'll have to clean up. Always be ready for the fallout.

Cybersecurity Relevance: Jimmy Burke's Lufthansa Heist was a flawless plan... until paranoia ripped it apart. Same thing happens in cybersecurity. You could pull off the perfect hack, but if you don't think about the aftermath, you'll watch your empire crumble from within. Hackers face the same heat. After the heist, it ain't just about the loot; it's about cleanin' up and makin' sure you don't get whacked by your own mistakes. Keep it tight, always have a plan for the fallout, and keep your crew loyal or you'll end up like those Lufthansa boys, lookin' over your shoulder.

4. The Demise of Bugsy Siegel

Benjamin "Bugsy" Siegel, a flamboyant gangster with charm and ambition, had a vision to build a gambling haven in the Nevada desert. This vision led to the creation of the Flamingo Hotel and Casino in Las Vegas.

The Plan: Siegel's dream was grand. The Flamingo would be the most luxurious casino-hotel, attracting Hollywood's elite and tourists from around the world. He convinced his mob associates to invest heavily, promising them a windfall once the casino was up and running.

The Punch: The Flamingo's construction was plagued with problems. Costs skyrocketed, and the project was way over budget. When the Flamingo first opened its doors in 1946, it was a disaster. The hotel wasn't finished, and the cold weather kept many patrons away. The casino lost $300,000 in the first week alone. That would be close to $4.25 million dollars today. The mob investors were not pleased. They had a plan for steady profits, but instead, they faced significant losses.

The final unexpected punch came for Siegel in 1947. As he sat in his Beverly Hills home, an unknown assailant fired multiple shots through the window, killing him instantly. It's widely believed that his mob associates ordered the hit due to the Flamingo's failures and suspicions that Siegel was skimming money. (biography.com, 2021)

Lessons Learned:

- **Unforeseen Challenges Can Derail a Perfect Plan**: Bugsy had the dream, the money, and the backing, but things still went south. Unexpected delays and spiraling costs sunk his Flamingo project.
  Lesson: In security or crime, even the best plans can be thrown off by things you didn't see coming. You gotta stay

flexible and always have a backup plan for when things go sideways.

- **You Need to Adapt Quickly When Problems Arise**: Bugsy should've jumped on the problems early, fixed what he could, and kept his backers happy. Instead, he let the issues pile up, and the result? A one-way ticket to an early grave.
  Lesson: If you don't adapt and fix problems fast, they'll bury you. Whether it's in business, construction, or cybersecurity, quick responses can turn a disaster into just a bump in the road.

- **Appearances Aren't Everything**: Bugsy's Flamingo was flashy, sure, but beneath the surface, it was a mess. Poor management, unfinished construction, and bad timing sealed its fate.
  Lesson: In both business and cybersecurity, having a flashy front means nothing if the foundation is weak. You can look good on the surface, but if your operations (or security) are a mess, it's all gonna fall apart.

Cybersecurity Relevance: Bugsy had big dreams with the Flamingo, but dreams don't protect you from bullets or from digital threats, for that matter. Bugsy's empire fell apart because of poor planning and bad management, just like when a business ignores cybersecurity. You might have a flashy website, but if your security's weak, one good hit and it's all gone, just like Siegel's luck in Vegas. Learn from ol' Bugsy, if you don't take cybersecurity seriously, you'll be out of the game faster than he was.

These tales from gangster lore emphasize the unpredictability of life in the underworld. Even with the best-laid plans, unexpected challenges can arise, and the consequences can be deadly. The same principle applies in the digital realm... always be prepared for the unexpected.

Till next time, keep your wits about you and your data locked up tight. Cheers!

Chapter 4: All I Do is Supply a Demand.

Now that you've been around the block and know a bit about Mr. Al Capone. Let me tell you what you need to know. The man was a legend in his own right, and one of his most famous lines was, "I am like any other man. All I do is supply a demand." At its core, this statement reflects a simple truth about human nature and the market forces that drive our actions.

Back in the day, during Prohibition, there was a demand for booze, and folks like Capone stepped in to supply it. Fast forward to today, and while the commodities have changed, the principle remains the same. In the realm of cybersecurity, there's a demand for certain... let's call them "illicit digital goods," and there are those who are more than willing to supply them.

The Demand: In today's interconnected world, information is power. Whether it's personal data, corporate secrets, or access to critical infrastructure, there's always someone willing to pay for unauthorized access. And where there's demand, there's opportunity for profit.

The Supply: Enter the hackers, the modern-day bootleggers of the digital age. These savvy individuals and groups craft malware, ransomware, and other malicious tools to exploit vulnerabilities in systems. Why? Because there's a market for it. Whether it's a competitor looking for an edge, a criminal organization seeking a ransom, or a nation-state aiming to gather intelligence, there's always someone willing to pay for these digital "goods."

Now, I ain't saying it's right. But just like in Capone's day, when there was a public outcry against alcohol but still a massive underground demand for it. Somebody's gonna fill that demand. Today's digital world presents a similar paradox. People decry hacking and cyberattacks, but the demand for these illicit services persists.

Your delivery is here. (Midjourney,, 2023)

So, what's a modern-day gangster to do in such a landscape? Here are a few lessons from the past:

- **Know the Market:** Just as Capone had his finger on the pulse of the speakeasy scene, today's cyber gangster needs to understand the digital black market. What are people paying for? What tools are in demand?

- **Trust is a Commodity:** In the underworld, trust is everything. Whether you're running a bootlegging operation or a digital heist, you need a crew you can rely on. Vet your associates carefully.

- **Stay One Step Ahead:** Law enforcement, both in the 1930s and today, is always evolving, always adapting. To stay out of the clink, you've got to be ahead of the curve. That means constantly updating your methods, tools, and techniques.

- **Know When to Walk Away:** Every gangster, whether in a pinstripe suit or behind a computer screen, needs to know when the heat is too much. If the risks outweigh the rewards, it might be time to lay low or get out of the game.

See here, I got a couple o' examples for ya.

1. The Rise of Ransomware-as-a-Service (RaaS)

In the modern cyber underworld, there's been a significant shift towards Ransomware-as-a-Service (RaaS). This model allows even those with limited technical skills to launch ransomware attacks, emphasizing the principle of "supplying a demand."

The Demand: A Thirst for Easy Money

In today's world, everything's digital—your photos, your money, even your grandma's secret cookie recipe. And where there's digital treasure, there are digital pirates. The demand for quick, easy money through ransomware attacks has skyrocketed. From city governments to healthcare systems, everyone's a target.

The Customer is Always Right

Back in my day, if people wanted booze during Prohibition, you gave 'em booze. If they wanted a place to gamble, you provided the tables. The customer is always right, even when the customer is on the wrong side of the law. The same principle applies to the modern cyber underworld.

The Art of Meeting the Demand

You see, not everyone's a computer whiz. But why should that stop them from joining the cybercrime wave? RaaS platforms have emerged to meet this demand, offering ready-made ransomware tools for the aspiring hoodlum. It's like buying a Tommy gun off the shelf, no questions asked.

The Supply: A Marketplace for Mayhem

Enter RaaS, the marketplace for mayhem. These platforms are the cyber equivalent of a back-alley arms dealer. They offer "off-the-shelf" ransomware tools that anyone can purchase or rent. You don't need to be a coding genius; you just need the guts to pull off the heist. And the best part? The providers take a cut, just like a mob boss taking his share of the loot. (cm-alliance, 2022)

The Art of Franchising Crime

What we're seeing here is the franchising of cybercrime. Just like a mob boss might franchise out his illegal operations to trusted associates, RaaS providers are franchising out cybercrime. They provide the tools and take a cut of the profits, while their "associates" do the dirty work.

Lessons Learned:

- **Democratization of Crime**: Back in the day, you needed muscle, know-how, and guts to pull off a heist. Now? Any schmuck with a laptop can get in the game thanks to RaaS. It's lowered the bar, lettin' more people take a swing at the cybercrime racket.
  Lesson: More criminals mean more attacks. Cybersecurity's gotta be tougher than ever, 'cause these digital goons are comin' outta the woodwork.

- **The Middleman Always Gets His Cut**: Just like in the old days, the guy providin' the tools is always takin' a piece of the action. RaaS providers give wannabe hackers the goods and take a cut of whatever they steal. It's a solid business model for criminals.
  Lesson: This setup fuels the fire, incentivizin' more hacks. The easier they make it, the more you're gonna need defenses that stand up to the onslaught.

- **Adapt or Perish**: The game's always changin', and cybercriminals know how to keep up. RaaS is proof that criminals evolve, just like we did back when the heat was on. If they can't get through the front, they'll find a way through the back.
  Lesson: You can't rest on your laurels. Keep your cybersecurity sharp, or you'll be yesterday's news. Always be a step ahead of the game, or you'll get left in the dust.

- **Know Your Enemy**: To win in this racket, you gotta know how the other side operates. RaaS runs like a well-oiled machine, supplying the tools and letting the small-time crooks do the heavy liftin'. Understand that, and you'll know how to fight back.

Lesson: If you know the enemy's playbook, you can build a better defense. Understanding RaaS helps create strategies that target vulnerabilities before they become a problem.

- **Regulatory Challenges**: Back when we ran speakeasies, the law had a tough time shuttin' us down. Same deal with RaaS platforms. They're hard to catch and harder to regulate, making it a real headache for the coppers.
  Lesson: Cybersecurity can't rely on laws alone to stop the bad guys. You need active measures, constant vigilance, and a strong digital presence to keep these platforms at bay.

- **The Ethical Dilemma**: It's easy to get your hands on ransomware these days, raisin' some big questions about the responsibilities of tech platforms. Just like back in the day when people questioned who was really runnin' the show, we gotta ask who's helpin' enable these crimes.
  Lesson: The tech world needs to take a good hard look at what they're makin' accessible. Closing off these avenues could slow down the wave of attacks.

Cybersecurity Relevance: Alright, here's the deal, see? Ransomware-as-a-Service is like when we sold protection back in the day. Only now, these cyber hoods are rentin' out their ransomware like it's a Tommy gun. This makes it easy for any two-bit hacker to get in on the action. In cybersecurity, it means more attacks, 'cause anybody with cash can get their hands on some serious firepower. You gotta keep your defenses strong, 'cause this racket? It ain't slowin' down.

So, whether you're a cybersecurity expert or a gangster from the golden age of crime, the lesson is clear: "I am like any other man. All I do is supply a demand." And in the world of RaaS, business is booming. Cheers!

2. The Sale of Zero-Day Exploits

Zero-day exploits, the lock-picks of the cyber underworld. These are the secret backdoors that let you waltz right into someone's digital life, no questions asked. These vulnerabilities in software that are unknown to the vendor, making them incredibly valuable in the cyber world. These exploits can be used to gain unauthorized access, deliver malware, or spy on users.

The Demand: The Unquenchable Thirst for Power

In the world of espionage, corporate warfare, and organized crime, knowledge is power. And what better way to get that knowledge than by sneaking into someone's system without them even knowing? Governments, corporations, and criminal organizations are always on the hunt for zero-day exploits. These digital skeleton keys can open doors that are supposed to be locked tight.

If There's a Market, Flood It

Back in the day, if people wanted illegal booze, you made sure you were the one to supply it. Today, if someone wants a zero-day exploit, there are those who will gladly provide. The market dictates the product, not the other way around.

The Art of Capitalizing on Secrecy

You see, the real art here is in the secrecy. Zero-day exploits are valuable precisely because they're unknown to software vendors. They're like the secret underground tunnels we used to smuggle booze during Prohibition—unknown to the cops and incredibly valuable to us.

The Supply: The Shadow Brokers of the Digital Age

Recognizing this insatiable demand, some hackers and even security researchers have turned into modern-day shadow brokers. Instead of reporting these vulnerabilities to be patched, they sell them to the highest bidder. There are even online platforms that act as middlemen, facilitating these transactions. Prices can go through the roof, with some exploits fetching millions of dollars. (Smeet, 2022)

Art of the Deal in the Cyber Underworld

These digital brokers negotiate the sale of zero-day exploits just like a mob boss negotiates deals and arranges transactions. They're the go-betweens, the facilitators of this dark trade. And just like any good middleman, they take their cut, skimming a little off the top for their troubles.

Lessons Learned:

- **The Ethics of Supply and Demand**: Just like we supplied illegal booze during Prohibition, there's always gonna be someone ready to supply zero-day exploits to the highest bidder. The market don't care about right or wrong, it cares about demand.
  Lesson: The sale of exploits creates a moral gray area. Hackers sell vulnerabilities for big bucks, but cybersecurity experts gotta decide—fix the problem or let the buyers run wild?

- **The Global Impact**: When we ran booze, we only messed with a few towns. But these exploits? They've got global reach. One crack in a system could bring down a whole company, or worse, a government.
  Lesson: These digital skeleton keys can affect more than just businesses. They can mess with governments, economies, and whole societies. Cybersecurity needs to think big.

- **The Arms Race**: Just like the Feds tried to shut down our speakeasies, the cybersecurity world tries to patch holes as fast as hackers find 'em. It's a never-ending back-and-forth, an arms race where the stakes keep gettin' higher.

Lesson: For every new defense, there's a new way to crack it. Cybersecurity is a game of cat and mouse, and it never stops.

- **Regulatory Challenges**: Back in our day, the law couldn't keep up with all our hideouts and tunnels. Now, regulators are playing catch-up with these exploit sellers. It's hard to pin down, and even harder to stop.
  Lesson: Just like Prohibition was tough to regulate, the sale of zero-day exploits is hard for the law to track. Cybersecurity teams gotta stay ahead of the game and not rely solely on legal protections.

- **The High Stakes**: Just like a big score during Prohibition could set you up for life, zero-day exploits are fetchin' millions. The stakes are higher than ever, attractin' all kinds of players, from lone hackers to state-sponsored operators.
  Lesson: High prices mean high risks. Cybersecurity experts are up against some serious players, and the payoff for hackers makes the fight even tougher.

- **The Role of Middlemen**: In our day, every deal needed a good middleman, someone to make sure the goods and the cash swapped hands smoothly. Same deal in the cyber world. These brokers handle the dirty work, keepin' the hackers and buyers in business.
  Lesson: Just like a good middleman in a mob deal, brokers in the zero-day market make it harder to track the source. Cybersecurity needs to be ready to deal with multiple layers of deception.

Cybersecurity Relevance: Zero-day exploits? These are the lockpicks of the digital age, kid. Just like how we had secret tunnels to smuggle booze back in Prohibition, these exploits open doors no one knows about. In cybersecurity, they're the Holy Grail for hackers, and when they hit the market, it's like a silent alarm goin' off. The folks in charge better stay sharp, 'cause once these skeleton keys get sold, your secrets are as good as gone.

These real-world examples highlight the principle that where there's demand, there will always be those willing to supply, regardless of the ethical or legal implications. The digital age has simply provided a new marketplace for age-old practices.

Here's a couple more for ya, kid.

3. The Numbers Game (or Policy Racket)

The Numbers Game, a classic from the golden age of gangsterdom. You see, before the government got its mitts on the lottery business, we had our own little operations. It was a simple game, but oh boy, did it rake in the dough. Let's delve into how this underground lottery was the epitome of "I am like any other man. All I do is supply a demand."

The Demand: The Dream of Easy Money

Back in the day, the working stiffs had it tough. Long hours, low pay, and not much to look forward to. But everyone's got dreams, right? Dreams of a better life, dreams of hitting it big without breaking a sweat. That's where the Numbers Games came in. For just a few pennies, you could bet on a three-digit number and hope lady luck was on your side.

If There's a Demand, Be the Supplier

Just like we supplied the booze during Prohibition, we supplied the dreams during hard times. The Numbers Game was a way for the common man to escape reality, if only for a moment. And where there's a demand for dreams, you can bet your last dollar we were there to supply it.

Exploits for Sale!! (Midjourney,, 2023)

The Art of Running the Game

The Numbers Game wasn't just about taking bets. Oh no, it was an operation, see? You needed runners to collect the bets, you needed a secure location for the draw, and you needed muscle to make sure no one tried to mess with your operation. It was a well-oiled machine, and it made us a fortune.

The Supply: The Mob's Lottery Empire

Recognizing the public's thirst for easy money, the mob took over the Numbers Game like a fish to water. We organized the bets, controlled the draws, and handled the payouts. And let's not forget, we took our cut... a generous one, I might add. The game was so lucrative that it led to turf wars among crime families. Control of this racket was worth its weight in gold. (wikipedia.org, n.d.)

The Art of Keeping the Peace

Now, running a successful Numbers Game wasn't just about taking bets and making money. It was also about keeping the peace. You see, when there's a lot of money involved, tempers flare and rivalries form. So, part of the art was in making alliances, cutting deals, and sometimes, settling scores to keep the operation running smoothly.

Lessons Learned:

- **The Ethics of Supply and Demand**: Just like with zero-day exploits, the Numbers Game was all about supplyin' what people wanted, even if it wasn't exactly legal. But was it right? That's the question, see? You're givin' people hope, but you're also takin' a cut.
  Lesson: In the racket, whether you're sellin' dreams or digital exploits, it's all about the balance between profit and morality. Just 'cause people want it doesn't make it right.

- **The Local Impact**: The Numbers Game wasn't just a city-wide thing, it ran deep in neighborhoods, affecting everything from crime rates to community loyalty. It kept folks hooked and drew in big players to keep the operation goin'.
  Lesson: Even a small-time racket can have big-time effects on communities, just like small-scale cyber scams today. Cybersecurity needs to focus on the ripple effect these scams have on a business and the public.

- **The Regulatory Challenge**: We ran the game until the government decided they wanted in. Once they saw how much money was being made, they set up their own lotteries. They took our racket and made it legit.
  Lesson: In cybersecurity, just like in the Numbers Game, regulation is always playin' catch-up. Hackers and crooks are always one step ahead of the law, so it's up to you to stay ahead of the game.

- **The High Stakes**: The Numbers Game wasn't for the faint of heart. With cash flowin' like water, it led to plenty of turf wars and bloodshed. You had to be tough to hold onto your piece of the pie.
  Lesson: When there's big money involved, the stakes rise fast. In cybersecurity, high-stakes operations like ransomware and data breaches lead to intense competition and some serious consequences.

- **The Role of Middlemen**: Just like in any good racket, middlemen were the ones makin' it all happen. The runners, the bookies, the muscle kept things movin' and made sure everyone got their cut.
  Lesson: Whether it's the Numbers Game or modern-day cybercrime, middlemen play a critical role. They make the connections between crooks and victims, and in cybersecurity, spotting these middlemen is key to cuttin' off the operation.

Cybersecurity Relevance: Ah, the Numbers Game, now that was a slick operation. Just like how we ran the policy racket, today's cybercriminals run digital lotteries and scams, preyin' on people's dreams of easy money. In cybersecurity, this applies to phishing schemes and frauds...simple, but effective. You protect yourself by stayin' vigilant and educatin' your crew on how to spot these scams before they make off with the loot.

So, whether it's the Numbers Game of yesteryear or the cyber rackets of today, the principle remains the same: "I am like any other man. All I do is supply a demand." And let me tell ya, business was always good. Cheers!

4. The O'Banion-Siegel Flower Shop Ruse

Ah, the O'Banion-Siegel Flower Shop Ruse, a classic tale of subterfuge and cunning. Dean O'Banion, that Irish charmer, ran a flower shop in Chicago, but don't let those roses fool ya. That shop was a front for all sorts of activities that were, let's say, less than legal. It's a perfect example of the principle, "I am like any other man. All I do is supply a demand."

The Demand: A Facade of Legitimacy

People love flowers, right? They buy 'em for weddings, funerals, and to say sorry when they've been a schmuck. So, a flower shop is the last place you'd suspect to be a hub of illegal activities.

But that's exactly what made it the perfect cover. The demand for flowers provided the ideal facade for O'Banion's real moneymaking schemes. (Jenkins, 2017)

The Gangster Wisdom: A Rose by Any Other Name
Dean O'Banion was no fool. He knew that to run a successful operation, you needed to keep the heat off. What better way to do that than to operate in plain sight? His flower shop was a legitimate business, but it was also the front for his bootlegging and racketeering operations.

The Art of the Double Life

Running a flower shop by day and a criminal empire by night takes a certain level of finesse. O'Banion had to balance his public persona as a respectable businessman with his underworld activities. He had to

73

keep his friends close but his enemies closer, always watching his back while maintaining a smile for the customers.

Just another delivery (Midjourney, 2023)

The Supply: More Than Just Bouquets

While the shop supplied flowers, O'Banion supplied much more. From the back rooms, he ran his operations, coordinating with other mobsters like Bugsy Siegel. They supplied what the public really wanted, booze during Prohibition, protection, and a little bit of vice.

The Art of Deception

Just like modern hackers use phishing websites that look legitimate to steal information, O'Banion used his flower shop to deceive the authorities. It was all about appearances. The shop had to look and feel legitimate to keep the coppers off his scent.

Lessons Learned:

- **The Power of a Front**: O'Banion's flower shop was the perfect cover. It was legit on the outside, but behind those roses, there was a whole lot more going on. The key was using the shop to keep the law from sniffin' around too much.
  Lesson: In the cyber world, phishing websites act the same way. They look clean, but they're hiding dirty business underneath. You gotta be sharp enough to spot the front, or you'll get burned.

- **Supplying Multiple Demands**: Sure, O'Banion was selling flowers, but that was just the window dressing. He was really supplying booze and protection, everything people needed but couldn't get legally.
  Lesson: In the cybercrime game, it's the same deal. Hackers don't just stop at one scam. They supply a range of illegal goods, ransomware, stolen data, and malware, always meeting the demand in the underground market.

- **The Importance of Appearances**: O'Banion's shop looked respectable, and that's what kept the coppers off his back for so long. It was all about looking legit while doing dirty work behind the scenes.
  Lesson: In cybersecurity, things that look harmless might be hiding a threat. You can't just judge by appearances, especially when it comes to seemingly innocent emails or websites that are phishing fronts.

- **The Complexity of Operations**: Running a flower shop by day and a bootlegging empire by night ain't simple, but O'Banion did it. Balancing two operations takes skill and planning. **Lesson**: Today's cyber crooks are doin' the same thing, runnin' complex scams behind legit-looking websites or businesses. You need a keen eye and strong defenses to uncover what's really going on.

- **The Ethical Dilemma**: Just because there's a demand doesn't mean you should supply it. O'Banion was meeting the demand for booze and protection, but at what cost? **Lesson**: In cybersecurity, this raises questions about ethics too. There's always a market for selling exploits or hacking tools, but doin' the wrong thing for a quick buck can lead to big problems down the line.

Cybersecurity Relevance: The O'Banion-Siegel Flower Shop, that was the front for everything dirty, just like today's phishing websites. The flower shop was legit on the surface, but behind the petals, it was a hub for all kinds of crime. Cybersecurity's got the same problem. What looks harmless might be a front for cyber crooks. You gotta dig deeper and make sure what you're dealin' with is the real McCoy, or you'll find yourself knee-deep in trouble.

So, whether you're peddling flowers or peddling malware, the game remains the same: "I am like any other man. All I do is supply a demand." And let me tell ya, in the world of crime, both digital and analog, demand is one thing you can always count on.

These examples from the world of organized crime underscore the principle that where there's a demand, especially for illicit or semi-illicit activities, organized crime will step in to supply. Whether it's offering a chance to gamble or finding ways to maximize and hide profits, the mob has always been adept at identifying and capitalizing on lucrative opportunities. As long as there's a market for illicit goods and services, there will always be those willing to provide them.

Till next time, keep your eyes open, your data secure, and always be wary of the digital shadows. Cheers!

Chapter 5: Trust is Good, But Control is Better, See?

Pull up a chair you dapper dames and dashing gents, light up a cigar, and let's talk turkey. You ever hear the saying, "Trust is good, but control is better"? Sure, it's a Russian proverb, but it fits the gangster mindset like a glove.

In the underworld, trust is a rare commodity. You might trust your crew, your family, maybe even your lawyer, but you always keep one eye open. Why? Because control is the name of the game. You can't just trust that things will go your way; you've got to make sure of it.

Same goes for cybersecurity, capiche? You can trust that your systems are as secure as Fort Knox, but that doesn't mean some wise guy won't try to crack it open. Trust is a good start, but it ain't the finish line. You gotta keep your eyes peeled and your ears to the ground. Trust is good, but it ain't foolproof.

Now, let's gab about control. In my racket, control is the name of the game. You control the booze, you control the money, you control the power. It's like holdin' all the aces in a deck of cards. And when you've got control, you don't have to rely on trust. You make your own luck, see?

In the world of ones and zeros, control means havin' the right security measures in place. We're talkin' firewalls, encryption, multi-factor authentication—the whole shebang. You wouldn't leave the vault to your speakeasy wide open, would ya? Nah, you'd have guards, locks, and maybe even a couple of German Shepherds named Bonnie and Clyde. That's control, baby!

Trust But Verify

Ah, but here's where the rubber meets the road. You gotta blend trust and control like a fine cocktail. Trust your people, but have controls in place to keep 'em honest. Trust your systems, but verify they're locked up tighter than Al Capone's vault. It's like havin' a loaded dice—you trust it'll land the way you want, but you've also rigged the game in your favor.

In cybersecurity, this means not just trustin' that your software is up to snuff, but also keepin' tabs on it. Regular audits, penetration tests, and keepin' up with the latest security patches—that's how you stay one step ahead of the coppers, er, I mean hackers.

Here's how you can apply some good ol' gangster wisdom to your cybersecurity practices:

- **Layered Security**: Think of this like having your own crew of bodyguards, each with a specific job. One guy checks for weapons, another keeps an eye on the crowd, and another watches the exits. In cybersecurity, this is akin to having firewalls, antivirus software, and intrusion detection systems working in tandem.

- **Regular Audits:** In the mob, you always have someone keeping the books, and you'd better check those numbers regularly to make sure no one's skimming. Similarly, regular security audits can help you identify any weaknesses before they become a problem.

Want'a play? (Midjourney, 2023)

- **Employee Training:** Even the most loyal soldier can mess up if he doesn't know what to look for. Training your team to recognize security threats is like teaching your crew how to spot a cop in plain clothes—it's essential for survival.

- **Incident Response Plan:** Every gangster knows you need a plan for when things go south—a getaway car, a safe house, and a plan to lay low. In the digital world, an incident response plan outlines the steps to take when a security breach occurs. Who gets notified, how to contain the threat, and how to recover—these are all part of a solid incident response plan.

- **Multi-Factor Authentication (MFA)**: Think of MFA like having multiple layers of security at the entrance of your secret hideout. One guy checks your ID, another scans for weapons, and a third makes sure you know the secret handshake. The more layers, the better.

1. Ransomware Attacks on Healthcare During COVID-19

Now we're talkin' about a real doozy—a tale of crime that hit when folks were already down on their luck. The COVID-19 pandemic was a tough time for everyone, but some lowlifes decided it was the perfect opportunity for ransomware attacks on healthcare systems. Let's see how this sordid tale fits into our guiding principle: "Trust is good, but control is better."

The Trust Game: Healthcare systems around the globe were overwhelmed, treatin' patients and tryin' to keep this virus at bay. They had to trust that their IT systems would hold up under the strain. After all, lives were at stake. Many healthcare providers also trusted that they wouldn't be targeted for attacks during a global health crisis. That's a gentleman's agreement, right?

The Control Factor: Well, not for everyone. Some cybercriminals took control of the situation in the worst way possible. They launched ransomware attacks, locking healthcare providers out of critical systems and demanding money to give control back. These criminals had their own form of control—over the data and systems they'd encrypted. Healthcare providers found that their trust in their existing cybersecurity measures was misplaced. They didn't have the control they thought they had. (Horowitz, 2021)

Trust But Verify: The attackers trusted their ransomware would do the job, and they verified its effectiveness by successfully locking out healthcare providers. On the flip side, many healthcare systems had antivirus software and firewalls they trusted, but they hadn't verified

81

that these measures would hold up under a targeted ransomware attack. They didn't have multi-layered security protocols, regular backups, or a disaster recovery plan that was up to snuff.

Cybersecurity Relevance: This example is a stark reminder that in cybersecurity, you can't afford to simply trust that you won't be targeted or that your existing measures are enough. You need to take control by constantly updating your security protocols, training your staff, and preparing for the worst-case scenario. In the world of cybersecurity, that means having a robust, multi-layered defense strategy that you regularly test and update.

Just like the other examples, the party that failed to maintain control ended up paying the price. In this case, the cost wasn't just monetary; it was potentially measured in human lives. So whether you're a healthcare provider, a financial institution, or just a regular Joe or Jane, remember: "Trust is good, but control is better."

Lessons Learned:

- **Control Means Being Prepared for the Worst:** Many healthcare providers lacked multi-layered security, regular backups, or disaster recovery plans. When their systems were locked, they had no control to restore operations.
  Lesson: Take control by preparing for the worst-case scenario. Implement multi-layered security measures, create regular backups, and ensure you have a tested disaster recovery plan.

- **Regularly Test and Update Security Protocols:** Healthcare systems relied on outdated antivirus software and firewalls, trusting that these measures were enough. They didn't test or update their defenses regularly, leaving gaps for attackers to exploit.
  Lesson: Regularly test and update your security protocols to keep up with evolving threats. Trust only what you have thoroughly tested and verified to be effective.

- **Training and Awareness are Crucial:**
  Ransomware attacks often succeed due to human error, such as clicking on phishing emails. Many healthcare providers likely lacked sufficient staff training on cybersecurity practices. **Lesson:** Ensure your team is trained and aware of the latest cybersecurity threats. Employees are often the first line of defense, and their knowledge and vigilance can make a big difference.

Cybersecurity Relevance: When healthcare was down during the pandemic, these cyber goons swooped in like vultures, takin' advantage of a bad situation. Ransomware attacks hit hospitals hard, cuttin' off access to critical systems and holdin' patient data hostage. In the world of cybersecurity, this attack showed that no one, not even the folks savin' lives, is off-limits. It's a cold reminder that vulnerability breeds opportunity—for both crooks and hackers. If you don't have control, you're left trustin' luck, and that ain't a good plan.

So, keep your guard up and your systems tighter than a drum. In this world, you can't afford to let your guard down, not even for a second. Cheers!

2. The Facebook–Cambridge Analytica Data Scandal

This one didn't involve Tommy guns or getaway cars, but lem'me tell ya, it was a caper that shook the world. Let's see how it fits into our golden rule: "Trust is good, but control is better."

The Trust Game: Facebook, the big kahuna of social media, had a lot of trust from its users. People willingly shared their likes, dislikes, political views, and even what they had for breakfast. Facebook also trusted third-party apps to play nice with its user data. Cambridge Analytica, a political consulting firm, seemed like just another player in the game.

The Control Factor: But here's where the plot thickens. Cambridge Analytica took control of the data from millions of Facebook users without their explicit consent. They used this data to influence political campaigns, including the 2016 U.S. presidential election. Facebook, on the other hand, had let its control measures slip. They trusted their third-party vetting process and their data-sharing policies, but they didn't have tight enough controls to prevent misuse.

Trust But Verify: Cambridge Analytica trusted that the data they harvested would give them the insights they needed to sway public opinion. And they verified this by testing their psychological profiles and targeted ads. Facebook, however, had trusted but not verified. They assumed their existing security and privacy measures were adequate. They didn't audit or monitor what third-parties like Cambridge Analytica were actually doing with the data. (Wong, 2019)

Cybersecurity Relevance: In the realm of cybersecurity, the Facebook–Cambridge Analytica scandal is a textbook example of what can go wrong when you trust without verifying. Trusting your security measures, your third-party partners, or even your users is not enough. You need to have controls in place to verify that the trust is warranted. That means regular audits, stringent third-party vetting, and real-time monitoring to catch any funny business before it turns into a front-page scandal.

Lessons Learned:

- **Don't Rely Solely on Trust**: Facebook trusted that its third-party apps, like Cambridge Analytica, would use user data responsibly. However, Cambridge Analytica exploited this data without user consent for political purposes.
  Lesson: Relying solely on trust can lead to misuse of data. It's important to actively manage and control who has access to sensitive information.

- **Lack of Control Over Third Parties**:
  Facebook didn't maintain strong oversight over third-party apps accessing its user data, allowing Cambridge Analytica to gather personal data without users' knowledge.
  Lesson: Maintain control over third-party access by implementing stricter vetting, audits, and real-time monitoring to ensure compliance with data usage policies.

- **Failure to Verify Leads to Exploitation**:
  Facebook failed to verify how Cambridge Analytica was using the data. Without auditing their actions, Facebook left a major gap in its security and privacy policies.
  Lesson: Always verify how your partners or third-party applications are using data. Regular audits and monitoring can prevent the misuse of sensitive information.

Cybersecurity Relevance: This one's a real slick scam, see? Facebook trusted too many shady characters with the keys to its kingdom, and Cambridge Analytica made off with all the loot...user data, that is. This scandal's a lesson that trustin' too much without proper oversight gets you burned. In cybersecurity, it's all about controlling who gets access and what they do with it. You let someone in the front door, and they'll clean out your safe if you ain't careful. It's not just about trust—it's about watchin' every move.

Each of these real-world examples underscores the importance of balancing trust with control. Whether it's trusting a social media platform with personal data or relying on a software vendor for critical network functions, these incidents show that control measures must be in place to verify that trust and protect against vulnerabilities.

3. The "Brink's Garage" Heist (1955)

Ah, the Brink's Garage Heist—a classic tale that even Hollywood couldn't dream up. It's a story that's got everything: cunning, betrayal, and a whole lotta dough. Let's dive in and see how it fits our motto: "Trust is good, but control is better." (www.fbi.gov, n.d.)

The Trust Game: In 1955, a group of eleven wise guys pulled off one of the most audacious heists in American history. They made off with $1.2 million in cash and $1.6 million in checks and other securities from the Brink's Garage in Boston. Now, Brink's trusted its security measures. They had a guarded facility, a reputation for being impenetrable, and the trust of the banks whose money they were safeguarding.

The Control Factor: But here's where it gets interesting. The gang didn't just waltz in and grab the loot. Nah, they spent two years planning this caper. They made copies of keys, studied the guards' routines, and even held dry runs. They took control of every variable they could. On the other side, Brink's had let their control measures slip. They trusted their reputation and their existing security protocols, but they didn't update or adapt them. They didn't have the control they thought they had.

Trust But Verify: The gang exploited this lapse in control. They struck when they knew the guards would be less alert, and they used their copied keys to bypass several layers of security. They trusted their plan but verified every detail, right down to the timing and the disguises they wore. Brink's, on the other hand, had trusted but not verified. They assumed their security was good enough; they didn't regularly update or test it.

Lessons Learned:

- **Control Requires Constant Vigilance:** The gang took control by carefully studying the guards' routines and vulnerabilities, whereas Brink's failed to adapt and maintain control over evolving risks.
  Lesson: Maintaining control means constantly assessing and

adapting your security measures to address potential new threats.

- **The Importance of Thorough Planning and Preparation:**
The gang spent two years meticulously planning the heist, making copies of keys, running dry runs, and studying every detail. Brink's, on the other hand, did not regularly test or update their security.
Lesson: Planning and preparation are essential for both criminals and defenders. Regularly testing and improving your security protocols is vital to staying ahead of potential attacks.

Nice Car (Midjourney, 2023)

- **Outdated Security Protocols are Weaknesses:** Brink's didn't update their security measures, relying on outdated protocols that the gang easily bypassed using copied keys and knowledge of guard routines.
  Lesson: Security measures need to be continuously updated. Outdated security leaves you vulnerable to attacks that exploit known weaknesses.

- **Testing is Essential:** The gang succeeded because Brink's didn't regularly test their security. They assumed it was sufficient, but the criminals knew otherwise.
  Lesson: Regularly test your security systems to identify and fix potential vulnerabilities. Complacency in security leads to breaches.

So, another lesson here is clear as gin: Trust in your security measures is all well and good, but taking control of every possible variable... that's where the real security lies. Whether you're safeguarding a million bucks or a million bytes, remember: "Trust is good, but control is better."

Cybersecurity Relevance: The Brink's Heist was one of the biggest scores in history, a real beauty of a job. But you know what made it possible? A lack of control. The crew cased the joint, copied keys, and studied every move. In cybersecurity, it's the same thing—if you ain't updating your systems or testing for weaknesses, you're handin' out keys to the vault. Hackers today use the same tactics, but instead of safes, they're after your data, and trust me, they're watchin' every gap you leave open.

Now, keep that in mind, and you'll avoid your own "Brink's Garage" moment, capiche? Cheers!

4. The Chicago Outfit's Control Over the Teamsters Union

Now we're gettin' into the nitty-gritty, the real meat and potatoes of organized crime. The Chicago Outfit—my kinda people—had their fingers in a lot of pies, but one of their most lucrative ventures was their control over the Teamsters Union. Let's see how this tale of power and influence fits our mantra: "Trust is good, but control is better." (SAMUELSON, 2022)

The Trust Game: The Teamsters Union was a big deal, representin' truckers and warehouse workers and wieldin' a lot of clout. Union leaders had to trust that their members would pay their dues and toe the line. Meanwhile, the rank-and-file trusted that the union would look out for their interests, negotiatin' for better wages and workin' conditions.

The Control Factor: Enter the Chicago Outfit. They didn't just wanna trust that the Teamsters would play ball. They wanted to control the game. Through a series of backroom deals, bribes, and the occasional strong-arm tactic, the Outfit gained significant influence over the union's pension funds and decision-making. They turned the Teamsters into a cash cow, fundin' everything from Las Vegas casinos to their own pockets. That, my friends, is control with a capital "C."

Trust But Verify: The Outfit trusted their inside guys in the union to keep the gravy train rollin', but they also verified. They kept tabs on union activities, made sure their interests were protected, and weren't afraid to step in when things didn't go their way. The Teamsters, on the other hand, trusted their leadership but failed to verify if that trust was misplaced. They didn't have the controls in place to prevent corruption at the highest levels.

Cybersecurity Relevance: In the digital world, this story serves as a warning about the dangers of not having proper oversight and control. You might trust your employees or even your leadership, but without checks and balances, you're open to internal threats. In cybersecurity terms, this could mean anything from insider trading based on stolen information to employees intentionally compromising systems or stealing data for personal profit.

Lessons Learned:

- **Trust Without Oversight Leads to Exploitation:**
  The Teamsters Union trusted their leadership without verifying their activities, which allowed the Chicago Outfit to infiltrate and take control for their own benefit.
  Lesson: Trusting your leadership or employees without oversight can lead to corruption and exploitation. Regular checks and controls are necessary to maintain integrity.

- **Internal Threats Can Be Just as Dangerous as External Ones:**
  The Teamsters didn't expect corruption to come from within their own ranks, but internal threats from leadership allowed the Chicago Outfit to infiltrate the union.
  Lesson: Internal threats can be just as dangerous as external ones. Always keep a close eye on insider activities and potential conflicts of interest to safeguard your organization.

- **Lack of Transparency Leads to Abuse:** The rank-and-file members of the Teamsters trusted their leaders but had no transparency into their decisions, allowing the Chicago Outfit to exploit the union's resources.
  Lesson: Ensure transparency in leadership decisions and financial processes. Lack of visibility allows for abuse, whether it's financial misconduct or other unethical behavior.

Cybersecurity Relevance: Now, the Chicago Outfit didn't just trust that the Teamsters would play along—they made sure of it, by takin' control of the union from the inside. In cybersecurity, you can't just trust your internal folks or partners to play nice. You gotta verify everything, run audits, and keep tight control. If you let an insider run wild without checks, you might find your whole operation under someone else's thumb, just like the Teamsters ended up under the Outfit's control.

Just like the Chicago Outfit took control of the Teamsters, a savvy hacker or even a disgruntled employee can take control of inadequately protected systems. And once they're in, they can do a lot of damage. So, whether you're running a union, a corporation, or a humble mom-and-pop shop, remember: "Trust is good, but control is better."

5. The Sicilian Mafia and the "Pizzo" Protection Racket

Let's take a little trip across the pond to sunny Sicily, where the olive trees grow and the Mafia knows how to run a business, if you catch my drift. In Sicily, the Mafia runs a protection racket known as the "Pizzo," where businesses are forced to pay a fee for "protection" against crime (often perpetrated by the Mafia themselves). This is a story that fits our golden rule like a glove: "Trust is good, but control is better." (Romano, 2007)

The Trust Game: In Sicily, many local businesses operate under the watchful eye of the Mafia. Now, these entrepreneurs must trust that paying the "Pizzo"—a protection fee—will keep their businesses safe from harm. It's an unspoken agreement: "You scratch my back, I won't break yours." The Mafia, in turn, trusts that these businesses won't go yappin' to the authorities.

The Control Factor: But let's not kid ourselves; this ain't about trust. It's about control. The Mafia controls the territory, the businesses, and even the local politicians to some extent. If you don't pay the "Pizzo," well, let's just say accidents happen. Fires, vandalism, you name it. The Mafia ensures they have control over the businesses, not just their trust.

We need to have a chat (Midjourney, 2023)

Trust But Verify: The Mafia doesn't just trust that businesses will pay up; they verify. Regular visits, subtle reminders, and less-than-subtle consequences ensure that everyone's keeping their end of the bargain. On the flip side, businesses may trust that paying the "Pizzo" will keep them safe, but they also verify by keeping a low profile and not attracting unwanted attention, which could jeopardize their "protection."

Cybersecurity Relevance: In the realm of cybersecurity, the "Pizzo" protection racket serves as a dark example of what can happen when one party has too much control without proper checks and balances. It's like giving one user or system administrator unchecked power over your network. Sure, you trust them now, but what happens if they go rogue? Or what if their credentials fall into the wrong hands?

Lessons Learned:

- **Unchecked Power Leads to Exploitation**:
  The Mafia controls the businesses, territory, and sometimes even the local politicians. This unchecked power allows them to exploit businesses through fear and manipulation.
  Lesson: Allowing any individual or group unchecked power over your systems or operations can lead to exploitation. Implement checks and balances to prevent abuse of power.

- **Layered Security Prevents Abuse**:
  Businesses in Sicily pay the "Pizzo" as a means of protection, but they lack other forms of security that could prevent Mafia interference. Without layered defenses, they are vulnerable.
  Lesson: Layered security such as multi-factor authentication, encryption, and role-based access control prevents abuse by ensuring that no single user has unrestricted access to critical systems.

- **Regular Audits and Monitoring are Essential**:
  The Mafia maintains control over the businesses through regular "check-ins" and consequences for non-compliance. Similarly, organizations must regularly audit and monitor their systems to ensure everything is functioning as it should.
  Lesson: Perform regular audits and real-time monitoring to ensure compliance with security protocols. Catching potential breaches early prevents major damage later on.

Cybersecurity Relevance: The Mafia in Sicily ran a neat little racket, collectin' protection money from local businesses. The "Pizzo" was all about control. They didn't just ask for trust, they enforced it with firepower. Cybersecurity's got its own version of the Pizzo, hackers demandin' ransom or threatenin' attacks if you don't pay up. It's a reminder that trustin' alone don't cut it; you need strong defenses in place to keep your data and systems safe from digital extortionists who'll bleed you dry if you let 'em.

Just like the Mafia maintains control through the "Pizzo," a hacker with unchecked access can exert control over your systems, data, and even your entire business. That's why it's crucial to have layered security measures, regular audits, and a system of checks and balances. Don't just trust that your systems are secure; take control to ensure that they are.

So, whether you're running a bakery in Sicily or a tech startup in Silicon Valley, the lesson is the same: "Trust is good, but control is better." Keep that in mind, and you'll be sittin' pretty, no matter what challenges come your way. Salute!

Each of these examples illustrates the delicate balance between trust and control in the world of organized crime. Whether it's pulling off a heist, running an illegal operation, or enforcing a protection racket, the key to success often lies in controlling the variables that you can't afford to leave to trust alone.

So, remember, trust might make the world go 'round, but control keeps it from spinning out of control. Whether you're running a bootlegging operation or safeguarding a corporate network, the principle remains the same: "Trust is good, but control is better."

Now, if you'll excuse me, I've got a high-stakes poker game to attend. And you can bet your bottom dollar I'll be bringin' both trust and control to the table. Cheers!

Chapter 6: You're Only as Good as Your Last Envelope

You ever hear the saying, "You're only as good as your last envelope"? In the mob world, that's a reminder that loyalty and payouts must be consistent. One mistake, one missed payment, and you're out of the family's good graces.

Now, what's this got to do with cybersecurity, you ask? Plenty, my friends, plenty. In the digital realm, you're only as secure as your last update or security audit. Just because you've been safe so far doesn't mean you can rest easy. The bad guys are always evolving, and if you're not keeping up, you're setting yourself up for a fall.

Here's how to keep your "envelopes" in check in the world of cybersecurity:

- **Regular Updates:** Think of software updates like those weekly envelopes full of cash. They're essential for keeping things running smoothly. Outdated software is a prime target for hackers, so make sure you're always running the latest versions.

- **Continuous Monitoring:** In the mob, someone's always keeping an eye on things to make sure no one's skimming off the top or planning a takeover. Similarly, continuous monitoring of your network can help you spot unusual activity before it becomes a full-blown breach.

- **Employee Training:** Loyalty in the mob isn't just about payouts; it's about trust and competence. Your employees need to be regularly trained to recognize threats like phishing scams and social engineering attacks. An educated team is a loyal and effective one.

- **Incident Response Drills:** Every good mobster has a plan for when things go south. Regularly testing your incident response plan through table-top exercises and drills can help you identify weaknesses and prepare your team for real-world scenarios.

- **Third-Party Audits:** Sometimes you need an outside perspective to see things clearly. Regular audits from third-party security experts can provide valuable insights into your security posture.

- **Zero Trust Architecture:** In the underworld, trust is a rare commodity. Adopting a zero-trust architecture—where you verify everything and trust nothing—can add an extra layer of security to your operations.

1. **T-Mobile Data Breach (2021)**

In August 2021, T-Mobile suffered a data breach that exposed the personal information of millions of customers.

The Last Envelope: T-Mobile, a major telecommunications company, had faced previous data breaches but had assured its customers that robust security measures were in place to protect their data. The company had invested in cybersecurity infrastructure and had a team of experts monitoring for threats. In other words, they had a good "last envelope," so to speak.

The Incident: In August 2021, T-Mobile suffered a significant data breach that exposed the personal information of millions of customers. The exposed data included names, Social Security numbers, phone numbers, and driver's license information. This was a massive blow to the company's reputation and raised questions about the effectiveness of its cybersecurity measures.

The Aftermath: The breach led to a flurry of legal and regulatory challenges for T-Mobile, not to mention the erosion of customer trust. The company offered free identity protection services to affected customers and vowed to enhance its cybersecurity measures. However, the damage was done, and the incident served as a stark reminder that past security measures were not sufficient. (Powell, 2023)

Lessons Learned:

- **Continuous Monitoring**: T-Mobile thought they had the joint locked up tight, but the crooks slipped in anyway. This shows that security ain't a one-time job; you gotta keep watchin' for new cracks in the wall. Cybersecurity needs round-the-clock surveillance, just like a smart boss always keeps his eyes on his territory.
  Lesson: In cybersecurity, you can't let your guard down. Keep those monitors runnin' and stay sharp for new threats. Vigilance is the difference between a tight operation and a busted one.

- **Data Encryption**: Look, when you're movin' sensitive stuff. Whether it's cash or customer info, you don't leave it out in the open. You lock it up tight. The T-Mobile job showed that data needs to be encrypted, both when it's sittin' still and when it's on the move.

Lesson: Encryption is like a safe. Even if someone gets past the front door, they can't crack what they can't see. Make sure your sensitive data's always protected, inside and out.

- **Incident Response**: When the heist goes down, you gotta be ready to act fast. T-Mobile was quick to respond, but they still got hit hard. Every outfit needs a plan in place for when things go sideways, or they'll be left pickin' up the pieces.
  Lesson: Have a tight incident response plan ready. You can't afford to be slow-footed when the hackers come knockin'. Speed and precision keep the damage under control.

- **Regulatory Compliance**: The law's always watching, just like the Feds keepin' tabs on the mob. T-Mobile's breach got people askin' whether they were keepin' up with the rules. You gotta stay ahead of regulations, or you'll find yourself in hot water with the law.
  Lesson: Stay on top of regulations and data protection laws. Compliance ain't optional, it's mandatory. Keep your operation legit, or the legal boys will have you up against the wall.

- **Customer Communication**: After the breach, folks were askin' questions, and T-Mobile wasn't quick enough with the answers. That's like keepin' your crew in the dark—never a good move. Clear, quick communication is key to keepin' your clients calm when the heat's on.
  Lesson: In the aftermath of a breach, communication is king. Let your customers know what's goin' on fast, or you'll lose their trust quicker than a two-bit hustler.

- **Third-Party Audits**: After takin' a hit like this, it's smart to call in outside help. Just like you bring in a neutral fixer to settle a beef, T-Mobile could've used an outside crew to audit their setup. An unbiased eye spots problems your own boys might miss.

Lesson: Don't be afraid to bring in third-party experts for an audit. They'll give you the straight dope on where your security's fallin' short, and that'll keep you from gettin' blindsided again.

Cybersecurity Relevance: The T-Mobile breach, see, was like leavin' the back door to the joint wide open. Millions of people's data— Social Security numbers, phone numbers, the whole shebang—was swiped, just like liftin' a payroll truck. In cybersecurity, this one reminds us that just 'cause you got locks on the front door don't mean your vault's safe. Data encryption and constant monitoring are your best pals here. Always keep an eye on your perimeter, or you'll find yourself payin' the price in more ways than one.

In summary, the T-Mobile data breach of 2021 serves as a warning that you're only as good as your last "envelope" in the realm of cybersecurity. Past successes and measures do not guarantee future security, and continuous updating, monitoring, and vigilance are crucial for maintaining a robust cybersecurity posture.

2. JBS Foods Ransomware Attack (2021)

In May 2021, JBS Foods, one of the world's largest meat processors, was hit by a ransomware attack that temporarily shut down some operations in Australia and North America.

The Last Envelope: JBS Foods, one of the world's largest meat processors, had cybersecurity protocols in place to protect its operations. The company had invested in firewalls, antivirus software, and other security measures to safeguard its systems. In essence, their "last envelope" seemed to be in good standing.

The Incident: In May 2021, JBS Foods fell victim to a ransomware attack that temporarily halted some of its operations in Australia and North America. The attack disrupted the meat supply chain, affecting both the company and consumers. The ransomware encrypted files on the company's servers, rendering them inaccessible and disrupting operations.

The Aftermath: JBS Foods took immediate action to contain the attack and initiated its incident response plan. The company also paid an $11 million ransom to the attackers to restore its systems, a move that generated significant debate about the ethics and implications of paying ransoms to cybercriminals. (Morrison, 2021)

Lessons Learned:

- **Incident Response Plan**: JBS had a plan in place, and they rolled it out quick when the attack hit. But the thing is, just havin' a plan ain't enough. You gotta keep that plan fresh, always testing it, 'cause the cyber landscape changes faster than a getaway car.
  Lesson: Keep your incident response plan up to date. It's like keepin' your getaway route mapped out. If you don't, you'll find yourself cornered when the heat comes down.

- **Continuous Monitoring**: These cyber crooks didn't just waltz in through the front door, they snuck in undetected. This is why keepin' an eye on your operations at all times is key. If you ain't watchin' for strange behavior on your networks, you won't see the hit comin' 'til it's too late.
  Lesson: Always keep your eyes on the system. Real-time monitoring is your lookout; without it, you're flying blind, and that's when the stick-up happens.

- **Employee Training**: Phishing scams and social engineering are like old-fashioned con games. These crooks slip in through an email, and next thing you know, your whole system's compromised. Training your crew to spot the grift is just as important as lockin' down the vault.
  Lesson: Educate your team. Every member's gotta know how

to spot a scam before it sinks the whole ship. One bad click, and you're in deep trouble.

- **Backup Systems**: JBS paid up to get their systems back, but if they had isolated backups, they coulda restored things without handin' over the cash. Backups are like hidin' a spare key. You only use it when you're locked out, but it saves your hide when things go south.
  Lesson: Have strong backup systems, separate from your main operations. If things get pinched, you can still recover without payin' off the crooks.

Noth'in to see here (Midjourney, 2023)

- **Supply Chain Security**: The JBS hit wasn't just about them. It rippled through the whole meat supply chain. Just like when a gang controls a whole neighborhood, one hit affects everyone. The cyber world's no different, and you gotta protect not just yourself but your whole network of suppliers.
  Lesson: Lock down your entire supply chain. A weak link in your partners can end up bein' your downfall, so make sure everyone you work with is buttoned up.

- **Regulatory Implications**: After the JBS attack, the Feds started lookin' into the security of critical infrastructure. This ain't just a small-time operation anymore. Big industries are under the microscope. You don't wanna be caught without the right protections when the regulators come knockin'.
  Lesson: Make sure you're playin' by the rules and meetin' regulations. If you ain't, the authorities will be on you faster than a raid.

Cybersecurity Relevance: JBS Foods got hit hard, like a meat racket gone sour. These cyber thugs held their systems for ransom, paralyzin' the supply chain. In cybersecurity, this is a classic stick-up—ransomware's a digital crowbar that cracks open your operations, bringin' the whole thing to a halt. The big lesson here? Backup systems and employee trainin'. You can't just rely on one set of books, ya need to keep duplicates off-site and make sure your crew knows how to spot a shady email before it slips past the defenses.

The JBS Foods ransomware attack in '21? It's a cold reminder that in this cybersecurity racket, you're only as good as your last envelope. Don't matter what you did yesterday, 'cause those past security tricks ain't gonna keep you safe tomorrow. The game's always changin', see? And if you ain't keepin' up, updating your defenses, checkin' your systems, and teachin' your crew to spot trouble, you're askin' for a hit.

Whether you're runnin' a big-time outfit or holdin' up critical infrastructure, you're only as safe as your last move. Just 'cause you got through one job clean don't mean you're safe from the next ambush. The cyber game's always movin', and if you wanna stay ahead, you gotta stay sharp, keep watch, and make sure your security is always one step ahead of the goons tryin' to take you down.

3. The Stardust Skimming Operation

The Stardust Casino, located on the Las Vegas Strip, was the epicenter of a notorious skimming operation in the 1970s and '80s. The casino was owned by the Argent Corporation, which was itself controlled by Allen Glick. However, the real power behind the scenes was Frank "Lefty" Rosenthal, who ran the casino operations. The skimming operation involved diverting casino profits away from the official books and funneling them to organized crime families in the Midwest, particularly the Chicago Outfit. (Bible, 2016) (Fischer, 2005)

The Last Envelope: For years, the operation was a massive success. Millions of dollars were skimmed and sent to mob families, ensuring loyalty and protection for those involved in the operation. The "last envelope," so to speak, was hefty and kept everyone content. The operation seemed foolproof, with casino employees, mob enforcers, and corrupt union leaders all playing their part to keep the money flowing.

The Downfall: Despite the operation's past successes, it eventually came crashing down. Several factors contributed to its demise:

- **Increased Law Enforcement Scrutiny:** As the FBI and other law enforcement agencies ramped up their efforts to combat organized crime, the Stardust became a target. Wiretaps, undercover agents, and informants began to infiltrate the operation.

- **Advancements in Surveillance Technology:** New methods of surveillance made it increasingly difficult to carry out the skimming operation without detection. The mob failed to adapt to these technological advancements.

I think I won! (Midjourney, 2023)

- **Internal Betrayals:** Trust within the operation began to erode. Some involved in the skimming started to cooperate with law enforcement, while others were suspected of skimming from the skim, leading to internal conflicts.

- **Public Exposure:** Media reports and public trials exposed the operation to the public, making it increasingly difficult to continue the skimming without attracting attention.

The Stardust skimming operation serves as a classic example of the principle that you're only as good as your "last envelope." The operation's past successes led to complacency. Those involved failed to adapt to new challenges, whether they were technological advancements, increased law enforcement scrutiny, or internal betrayals. They relied too much on their past successes, thinking they were invincible, and failed to update their "security measures" to protect against emerging threats.

In the end, several key figures were indicted, and the operation was dismantled, leading to significant legal repercussions and the end of an era for the mob's influence in Las Vegas. The Stardust itself was eventually sold to new owners and was imploded in 2007 to make way for new developments, marking the definitive end of its notorious past.

In the end, several key figures were indicted, and the operation was dismantled, leading to significant legal repercussions and the end of an era for the mob's influence in Las Vegas. The Stardust itself was eventually sold to new owners and was imploded in 2007 to make way for new developments, marking the definitive end of its notorious past.

Lessons Learned:

- **Complacency Leads to Failure:** The Stardust skimming operation was highly successful for years, but its success led to complacency, with key figures failing to adapt to changing circumstances.
  Lesson: Relying on past success can make you vulnerable. Constant vigilance and adaptation are necessary to stay ahead in any operation, especially when the stakes are high.

- **Audits and Continuous Monitoring are Key in Cybersecurity:**
  Just as law enforcement eventually caught on to the Stardust
  skimming operation, today's cybersecurity threats often
  involve data or financial skimming that can go undetected
  without proper audits and monitoring.
  Lesson: Continuous monitoring and regular audits are
  essential in both physical and digital security. In cybersecurity,
  this means staying alert for subtle changes or anomalies that
  could indicate a long-running breach.

Cybersecurity Relevance:

The Stardust skimming was a beautiful scam, mobsters siphoning
profits right outta the casino, undetected for years. Today's hackers
use the same tactics in the digital world, skimming data and money
over time without setting off alarms. Cybersecurity's lesson? Don't
get too comfy. Continuous audits and vigilance are key. Just like the
Feds eventually caught on to the skim, one slip in monitoring and
your operation's over.

4. The Castellammarese War - The Legacy of the Envelope:

Listen up, pal. The Castellammarese War, see, it's named after that
Sicilian town, Castellammare del Golfo. That's where a lot of the big
shots came from, got it? It was a big deal for us wiseguys in the
American Mafia. It raged from 1930 to 1931 and flipped our world
upside down in the United States.

Now, during this ruckus, the "envelope" was still the name of the
game. You pay up the ladder, capisce? It showed who was loyal, who
had respect, and who had the muscle. Miss a payment, and you'd be
swimming with the fishes. Pay on time, and you're solid. This war,
with all its backstabbing and power plays, is a prime example of the
cutthroat life we lead in this business. It's a constant shuffle for
power.

The roots of this war? They go back to rivalries from the old country, Sicily. Joe "The Boss" Masseria and Salvatore Maranzano, two big cheeses, ended up on opposite sides. Masseria ruled Manhattan, he was the top dog. Maranzano, he was the new blood from Castellammarese, looking to take over.

The roots of this war? They go back to rivalries from the old country, Sicily. Joe "The Boss" Masseria and Salvatore Maranzano, two big cheeses, ended up on opposite sides. Masseria ruled Manhattan, he was the top dog. Maranzano, he was the new blood from Castellammarese, looking to take over.

How you doin? (Midjourney, 2023)

Prohibition made us rich, and everyone wanted a cut. By the end of the '20s, tensions were hotter than a jalapeño. Both sides started arming up, and New York turned into a war zone.

The first big hit was Gaetano Reina in 1930. He was tight with Masseria, but when he got clipped, it left a big opening. Both sides wanted a piece of his racket.

Then there was Ciro Terranova, the "Artichoke King." He was with Masseria at first, but then he switched sides. Shows you how slippery alliances were back then.

Lucky Luciano was a key player. He was with Masseria but got sick of the old ways. He teamed up with Maranzano and took out Masseria in April '31 at a joint in Coney Island. But Luciano was no fool. He saw Maranzano's move to become the top boss and had him whacked on September '31.

After the dust settled, both Masseria and Maranzano were pushing up daisies. Luciano and his pals, like Meyer Lansky and Bugsy Siegel, reshaped the Mafia. They set up the "Five Families" and the Commission to keep things in line and avoid more bloodbaths.

Lessons Learned:

- **Old Ways Can Lead to Demise:** Lucky Luciano grew tired of Masseria's old ways and sided with Maranzano to take him out. However, when Maranzano tried to become the top boss, Luciano had him killed too, signifying a shift to a more modern, organized structure for the Mafia.
  Lesson: Sticking to outdated methods can lead to failure, especially when newer, more effective ways emerge. Adapting and evolving is essential for survival in any business or operation.

- **Opportunism Thrives During Chaos:** The war created opportunities for those who played their cards right, like Lucky Luciano, who took advantage of the chaos to reshape the Mafia's structure with the Five Families and the Commission.
Lesson: In times of chaos or transition, opportunists can emerge to gain control. Knowing when and how to seize opportunities while avoiding the pitfalls of chaos can lead to success.

- **Protect Your Territory:** Just as Mafia factions fought to control territories, in cybersecurity, different hacker groups fight for control of systems. Staying vigilant, protecting assets, and avoiding internal conflicts are crucial to defending against attacks.
Lesson: In cybersecurity, it's important to maintain strong defenses, monitor for potential threats, and stay proactive to prevent external threats from taking control of your systems.

Cybersecurity Relevance: The Castellammarese War? That's what happens when rival factions try to muscle in. In cybersecurity, it's like different hacker groups fighting for control of your systems. Each faction lookin' to take over the territory, and if you ain't careful, you'll be caught in the crossfire. Protect your organization like a tight-knit crew. Keep everything locked down and always be ready for a digital ambush.

In hindsight, the Castellammarese War was all about double-crosses, alliances, and power grabs. Loyalty in this racket is as fickle as the weather. Today's friend is tomorrow's enemy. The envelope? It may not always be going to the same place, but somebody is always waiting for it... and don't you fugitabout it.

5. **The Meteoric Rise and Catastrophic Fall of Dutch Schultz**

Hey kid, Dutch Schultz, real name Arthur Flegenheimer, wasn't just some two-bit hustler. He was the real deal, a symbol of the wild power shifts in the underworld of the '20s and '30s. His tale, full of ambition, paranoia, and backstabbing, nails the saying, "You're only as good as your last envelope."

From Rags to Riches: Born to German-Jewish immigrants in the Bronx, Schultz started small-time as a burglar. But when Prohibition hit, he saw his golden ticket in bootlegging. With a mix of muscle and smarts, Schultz took over the beer racket in the Bronx. Before long, he was pulling in over $20 million a year – serious dough back then.

The Envelope Game: In our line of work, paying up the chain is sacred. It's not just about the cash; it's about respect, loyalty, and keeping your back covered. Schultz knew this game well, making sure his bosses got their cut. Those envelopes stuffed with greenbacks bought him a lot of protection from the big boys.

The '30s brought tough times. When Prohibition ended in '33, Schultz's bootlegging empire took a hit. But he wasn't one to quit. He jumped into the numbers racket in Harlem, but that put him at odds with the Italian Mafia, who wanted in on the action too.

Then there was Thomas E. Dewey, a prosecutor with a bone to pick. Dewey was gunning for the top mobsters, and Schultz was on his radar. Feeling the heat, Schultz cooked up a plan to whack Dewey. In his mind, taking Dewey out would solve all his problems.

The Mafia Commission, the mob's top council, thought Schultz was nuts. They knew offing Dewey would bring down a storm of law enforcement on them. Schultz's refusal to back down was a big no-no. His trusty envelopes couldn't save him this time.

In 1935, at a joint in Newark, New Jersey, Schultz met his end. The Commission sent two hitmen to take care of business, and Schultz was history. That night marked the fall of one of the most notorious gangsters of the time.

Lessons Learned:

- **Taking Unnecessary Risks Can Lead to Ruin**: Schultz's plan to assassinate prosecutor Thomas Dewey was seen as reckless by the Mafia Commission. The unnecessary risk of bringing heat from law enforcement led the Commission to turn on him. **Lesson**: Taking unnecessary or overly ambitious risks, especially when advised against them, can lead to your downfall. It's important to evaluate the consequences of your actions carefully before making bold moves.

- **Evolve or Fall Behind**: Schultz's downfall mirrors what happens when businesses don't evolve in the cybersecurity world. Just as Schultz didn't see the risks that would destroy him, companies that don't stay updated on cybersecurity threats will face breaches and attacks. **Lesson**: In cybersecurity, staying ahead of the game is crucial. Regularly updating defenses, monitoring for threats, and training staff to stay informed can prevent a sudden collapse.

Cybersecurity Relevance: Dutch Schultz was ridin' high 'til his empire crumbled around him, takin' too many risks and gettin' sloppy. In cybersecurity, this is what happens when you don't evolve—today's protections can be tomorrow's weaknesses. Dutch didn't see his downfall comin', and neither will you if you don't keep your defenses updated and your team trained. One day you're on top, the next, you're pickin' up the pieces.

Dutch Schultz's life shows how fickle power is in the gangster's world. No matter how high you climb, you're bound to fall if you don't play by the rules. Schultz's story is a grim reminder that in organized crime, loyalty is slippery, and sometimes that last envelope might not be enough. (www.legendsofamerica.com, n.d.)

These examples from the world of organized crime and gambling illustrate the principle that you're only as good as your last "envelope." Whether it's maintaining the loyalty of your crew, adapting to new challenges, or ensuring your operations are secure from both internal and external threats, past successes offer no guarantees for the future.

So, remember, folks, in cybersecurity, as in the mob, you're only as good as your last envelope. Past successes don't guarantee future security. The threats are always evolving, and you've got to evolve with them if you want to stay ahead of the game.

Till next time, keep your software updated, your eyes open, and your data locked down. Cheers!

Chapter 7: This is Nothing Personal, It's Strictly Business

Ah, "The Godfather," a cinematic masterpiece that captures the essence of organized crime. Remember that golden line? "This is nothing personal, it's strictly business." It's like poetry for us underworld folks. You see, in our world, whether you're running illegal casinos or smuggling liquor, it's not about grudges or personal vendettas...most of the time. We all try to keep it about maximizing profits and staying ahead of the game.

Now, let's jump forward a few decades to this thing they call "cybersecurity." You might be surprised to learn that hackers and cybercriminals operate on the same principle most of the time. They're not breaking into systems because they've got a bone to pick with you. Nah, they're in it for the money or some other strategic goal. It's all business, baby, just like the rackets we used to run.

The Many Faces of Profit-Driven Cyberattacks

- **Ransomware: The Digital Kidnapping:** Imagine you wake up one day, and boom! All your files are locked up tighter than Al Capone's vault. That's ransomware for you. Hackers encrypt your data and won't give you the key unless you pay up. It's the 21st-century version of a kidnapping racket, and the criminals don't care who you are; they just want the ransom.

- **Data Breaches: The Virtual Bank Heists:** The good ol' days of bank heists, where you'd crack a safe and make off with bags of cash. Well, data breaches are the modern equivalent. Hackers break into systems to steal valuable information— credit card numbers, passwords, you name it—and then sell it on the dark web. It's a high-stakes game with a digital getaway car.

- **Cryptojacking: The Silent Siphon:** Remember how we used to siphon gasoline back in the day? Cryptojacking is the digital version. Hackers use your computer's processing power to mine cryptocurrencies like Bitcoin, all without you even knowing. It's like stealing someone's go-go juice to fuel your get-away car.

- **Corporate Espionage:** Back in my day, we'd sabotage a rival gang's operations to gain an edge. Corporate espionage is the white-collar version. Companies hack into each other's systems to steal trade secrets or get a leg up in the market. It's all about gaining territory, but in a digital landscape.

- **Political Hacking: The Game of Influence:** Ah, politics, the dirtiest game in town. Political hacking aims to influence public opinion or even election outcomes. It's like when we used to pay off politicians to turn a blind eye to our operations, but now it's done through social media manipulation and data leaks.

- **Denial of Service Attacks: The New-Age Turf War:** Imagine shutting down a rival's speakeasy for a night. That's what a Denial of Service (DoS) attack does to a website. It overwhelms the site with traffic, making it inaccessible. It's not about making money; it's about asserting dominance and disrupting the competition.

1. Equifax Data Breach — The Modern-Day Stardust Operation

In September 2017, Equifax, one of the largest credit reporting agencies in the United States, announced a data breach that had occurred between mid-May and July of the same year. The breach exposed the personal information of 143 million Americans, including Social Security numbers, birth dates, addresses, and in some cases, driver's license numbers. Additionally, credit card numbers for about 209,000 U.S. consumers were also accessed. The breach was a massive violation of privacy and put millions at risk of identity theft and financial fraud.

The Nitty-Gritty: How It Happened

The breach was attributed to a vulnerability in a website application framework that Equifax used. Despite patches being available to fix this vulnerability, Equifax failed to implement them in time, leaving their systems exposed. Once the hackers found this weak spot, they were able to infiltrate the system and gain access to a treasure trove of personal data. It was a failure of cybersecurity measures on multiple levels, from not updating software to not detecting the intrusion in time.

The Fallout: Repercussions and Consequences

The aftermath of the Equifax breach was severe. The company's stock price plummeted, and it faced numerous lawsuits, not to mention the loss of consumer trust. People affected by the breach had to freeze their credit reports and monitor their financial accounts for suspicious activities, a process that was both time-consuming and stressful. The breach also led to regulatory scrutiny and calls for stricter data protection laws. (archive.epic.org, n.d.)

Another day at the Casino (Midjourney, 2023)

Lessons Learned:

- **Always Patch Your Vulnerabilities**: Look, kid, you don't leave the back door to the joint wide open, capisce? Equifax did just that when they didn't patch a security hole that had a fix ready to go. In our world, you'd be a fool to not lock up after yourself. In cybersecurity, patchin' those vulnerabilities is like lockin' the vault. You don't do it, you're askin' to get hit. **Lesson**: Keep your systems up to date. A small crack in your defenses can let the whole operation come crashing down. Patch every hole before the bad guys slip in.

- **Be Vigilant**: Any wise guy knows you gotta keep your eyes peeled at all times. You let your guard down, and the coppers or the competition will be all over you. Equifax didn't keep a close watch on their systems, and by the time they knew they were hit, it was already too late. Same goes for cybersecurity. If you ain't watchin', you're beggin' to get knocked over.
  Lesson: Never get comfortable. Constant monitoring of your systems is the only way to catch intruders before they walk off with your valuables.

- **The High Cost of Failure**: In the mob, screw-ups cost you more than a few bucks; they could cost you your life. For Equifax, the price was steep. Stock prices plummeted, lawsuits came flyin', and trust? Forget about it. You slip up like that in cybersecurity, and the fallout could cripple your operation, just like a botched job would ruin a crew.
  Lesson: One mistake can sink the whole operation. Whether you're in the streets or in cyberspace, failing to protect your assets can lead to massive losses—money, reputation, and trust.

Cybersecurity Relevance: The Equifax data breach? Kid, this was the big one, 143 million records, snatched like it was nothin'. It's like the Stardust skim, only digital. They left the door unlocked, and the crooks waltzed in, takin' names, Social Security numbers, and credit cards. In cybersecurity, this is a warning shot, patch your holes or pay the price. Just like in the old days, you gotta keep your vault secure, or someone else will be walkin' off with the goods.

The Equifax data breach serves as a cautionary tale that emphasizes the importance of robust cybersecurity measures and the high stakes involved in protecting valuable assets, be it cash in a casino or data in a digital vault.

2. Marriott Data Breach — The Modern-Day Skimming Operation

In November 2018, Marriott International, one of the world's largest hotel chains, announced a massive data breach affecting up to 500 million customers. The breach exposed a variety of personal information, including names, addresses, phone numbers, email addresses, passport numbers, and even credit card information. The breach had been ongoing since 2014, but it wasn't discovered until four years later, making it one of the most significant and prolonged data breaches in history.

The Nitty-Gritty: How the Marriott Breach Happened

The breach was traced back to the Starwood guest reservation database, a system Marriott had acquired in 2016. The attackers had unauthorized access to the Starwood network since 2014, two years before the acquisition. They used this access to siphon off customer data over an extended period, effectively "skimming" valuable information that could be sold or exploited later.

The Fallout: Reputational and Financial Damage

The Marriott data breach had severe consequences for the company, both in terms of reputation and finances. Marriott faced regulatory fines, including a hefty £99 million penalty from the UK's Information Commissioner's Office. The breach also eroded customer trust, with many questioning the company's ability to safeguard their data. (Perlroth, Tsang, & Satariano, 2018)

The Skimming Operation Analogy

In the criminal underworld, a skimming operation involves siphoning off money or valuable goods gradually, often without immediate detection. The Stardust Casino skimming operation, for example, saw mobsters slowly funneling off casino profits to avoid detection. Similarly, the Marriott data breach involved the slow and steady extraction of customer data, making it a modern-day skimming operation.

Lessons Learned:

- **Long Cons Require Long Vigilance**: In our line of work, pulling off a skim means keepin' it quiet, spreadin' it out over time so nobody notices. The same goes for these cyber crooks. Marriott got hit over four years, and they didn't catch on till it was too late. A breach like this is a long con, and just like back in the day, you gotta be constantly watchin' your books to catch it early.
  Lesson: Constant vigilance is key. Don't think just because nothin' looks wrong today, you're safe. Keep an eye on the books—both your ledgers and your logs—so you spot the crooks before they clean you out.

- **The Bigger the Operation, the Bigger the Risk**: Just like the biggest casinos attract the biggest skimming operations, big companies like Marriott are prime targets for these data thieves. The more you've got, the more you've gotta protect. And let's face it, when you're running a joint that big, there are more doors to lock, more cracks to fill, and more eyes you gotta have on the place.
  Lesson: If you're a big fish, you're in a bigger pond with bigger sharks. Scale your security to match your operation, or you'll find out the hard way that more money means more problems.

- **Due Diligence in Acquisitions**: When you're movin' into new territory, you always check it out first. You don't take over a racket without knowing who's been workin' it and what problems come with it. Marriott bought Starwood, but they didn't check under the hood. That ongoing data breach was a time bomb they didn't see coming.
  Lesson: Always do your homework before acquiring anything. Dig deep into the cybersecurity health of any new acquisition, or you could end up buying more trouble than it's worth.

- **The Aftermath is Just the Beginning**: When a skim gets discovered, that's just the start of the mess. You've got lawmen sniffing around, and the fallout can last for years. Same with data breaches. Marriott's troubles didn't end when they found the breach; the lawsuits, fines, and lost trust were just the beginning of their headache.
Lesson: Discovering a breach is just the start of your problems. Be prepared for the long haul with legal issues, financial losses, and the uphill battle to rebuild trust with customers.

Cybersecurity Relevance: Marriott...they got hit slow and steady, just like we used to skim off the top. Four years those hackers were workin' the angle, siphoning off customer info like it was pocket change. In cybersecurity, this shows ya gotta be vigilant, always lookin' for small leaks before they turn into a flood. Long cons are a cybercriminal's bread and butter, so you need constant surveillance or risk bleedin' out before you even know it.

So there you have it. The Marriott data breach serves as a cautionary tale that in the digital age, skimming operations have evolved but are just as damaging. Whether it's siphoning off casino profits or stealing customer data, the essence remains the same: unauthorized entities taking what doesn't belong to them for financial gain. And as always, it's never personal; it's strictly business.

3. The Kray Twins — The Art of Manipulation

Reggie and Ronnie Kray, better known as the Kray Twins, were infamous gangsters who ruled London's East End in the 1950s and 1960s. They were involved in various criminal activities, from armed robbery to murder. However, what set them apart was their unique ability to manipulate people. They used a combination of charm, charisma, and intimidation to get what they wanted. Whether it was coercing a business owner into paying protection money or manipulating politicians and law enforcement, the Krays were masters of social engineering in the criminal world. (Campbell, 2015)

The Nitty-Gritty: How the Krays Operated

The Krays had a knack for understanding human psychology. They knew when to be charming and when to be intimidating. They would often start with charm, wining and dining their targets, making them feel special and valued. If that didn't work, they weren't above using threats and violence to achieve their goals. Their ability to read situations and people made them incredibly effective and dangerous.

The Fallout: The End of an Era

The Kray Twins were eventually arrested and convicted, but their legacy lived on. They became a symbol of how far one could go by manipulating people, a lesson not lost on future generations of criminals. Their story has been the subject of numerous books, movies, and documentaries, each dissecting their unique blend of charm and ruthlessness.

The Dark Art of Social Engineering

In the realm of cybersecurity, social engineering attacks aim to manipulate individuals into divulging confidential information, such as passwords or financial details. These attacks often start with research on the target, followed by carefully crafted phishing emails or direct interactions designed to exploit human psychology. Just like the Krays used charm and intimidation, social engineers use various tactics, from posing as trusted figures to creating a sense of urgency, to manipulate their targets.

The Nitty-Gritty: How Social Engineering Works

Social engineering attacks often begin with information gathering. Cybercriminals may stalk social media profiles, company websites, or other public sources to gather information about their targets. Armed with this information, they craft convincing narratives to trick individuals into revealing sensitive data. The attack could be as simple as a phishing email claiming to be from a trusted source or as complex as a voice phishing (vishing) attack where the attacker impersonates a company executive over the phone.

Can someone pass me the salt? (Midjourney, 2023)

The Fallout: A Growing Threat

Social engineering remains one of the most effective hacking techniques because it exploits human weakness rather than technological vulnerabilities. The consequences can be devastating, leading to financial loss, data breaches, and severe reputational damage for the affected individuals or organizations.

Lessons Learned:

- **Know Your Target**: The Krays didn't just roll up on someone without knowing the lay of the land. They studied people, found out what made 'em tick, and used that knowledge to their advantage. Same goes for social engineers today—they research their targets, learning personal details to exploit vulnerabilities.
  Lesson: Always assume someone's scoping you out, whether it's an underworld boss or a hacker. Be cautious about what info you put out there and train your crew to do the same.

- **Adapt Your Approach**:
  Reggie and Ronnie were masters at reading the room. They'd charm you with a smile or knock you down with a fist, depending on what the situation called for. Social engineers are no different. They adapt based on how you respond, using charm or urgency to get what they need.
  Lesson: Whether it's in business or cybersecurity, keep your guard up. Always be aware that people might change their tactics if the direct approach doesn't work.

- **Never Underestimate Human Psychology**:
  The Krays didn't need fancy gadgets or big operations. They knew human behavior inside and out. Social engineers today work the same angle. They play on fear, greed, or urgency to get someone to hand over valuable info.
  Lesson: Build cybersecurity with the human element in mind. Teach your team that no system's safe if the weakest link, the human, isn't trained to spot manipulation.

- **Consequences are Far-Reaching**:
  The Kray Twins' manipulation wasn't just about one quick

score; the ripples of their actions spread far and wide. In cybersecurity, social engineering attacks can have long-lasting consequences, financial losses, reputational damage, and worse.

Lesson: The fallout from manipulation lasts long after the initial breach. Always have backup plans and be prepared for the long-term effects of a data or security breach.

Cybersecurity Relevance: The Kray Twins, masters of manipulation. They knew how to charm ya, then squeeze ya. In cybersecurity, social engineering works the same way: charm 'em with a phishing email, then rob 'em blind. The Krays didn't need tech, just psychology. Hackers today use the same tools to get in through the front door. It's not about breakin' in anymore; it's about gettin' people to hand over the keys.

There you have it, capishe? The Kray Twins and social engineering attacks serve as a compelling study in the art of manipulation. Whether it's the gritty streets of 1960s London or the digital highways of the internet, the game remains the same: exploiting human weaknesses to achieve nefarious ends.

4. The Purple Gang's Bootlegging and Software Piracy

The Purple Gang, based in Detroit during the Prohibition era, was a notorious criminal organization primarily involved in bootlegging. They smuggled alcohol from Canada into the United States and distributed it through a network of speakeasies and other illegal venues. The gang was ruthless, eliminating competition through intimidation and violence. They were so effective that they virtually monopolized the alcohol trade in Detroit for several years.

The Nitty-Gritty: How the Purple Gang Operated

The Purple Gang's operations were a masterclass in logistics and distribution. They had a network of boats and trucks for smuggling, warehouses for storage, and a distribution system that could deliver alcohol to any part of the city on demand. They also had law enforcement and politicians on their payroll, ensuring that their operations ran smoothly with minimal interference.

The Fallout: The End of an Era

The Purple Gang's reign came to an end as Prohibition was repealed and as internal strife weakened the organization. However, their methods of illicit distribution left a lasting impact on organized crime, illustrating how a well-organized network could effectively monopolize an illegal commodity. (Kavieff, n.d.)

Cybersecurity Parallel: Software Piracy, The Digital Bootlegging

In the digital age, software piracy has become the modern equivalent of bootlegging. Just like the Purple Gang smuggled alcohol, today's cybercriminals distribute illegal copies of software across the globe. These pirated versions often come without the security features and updates provided by legitimate versions, making them a cybersecurity risk.

The Nitty-Gritty: How Software Piracy Operates

Software piracy often involves sophisticated networks of distribution. Pirated software can be found on peer-to-peer networks, illegal download sites, and even sold on the dark web. The operation often involves cracking the software to bypass security features and then distributing it through various channels.

The Fallout: A Persistent Problem

Software piracy continues to be a significant issue, costing the industry billions of dollars annually. It also poses a security risk, as pirated software can be a vector for malware and other cybersecurity threats. Efforts to combat software piracy often involve legal action, public awareness campaigns, and technological countermeasures like more robust software protections.

Lessons Learned:

- **Distribution is Key**:
  The Purple Gang controlled the booze biz because they had a top-notch distribution network. Boats, trucks, warehouses, they had it all. Same goes for software pirates today, pushin' illegal programs all over the globe. Whether it's bootleg booze or cracked software, distribution makes or breaks the operation.
  Lesson: In cybersecurity, keeping a tight rein on your distribution channels is crucial. Whether it's legitimate software or sensitive data, if you don't control the flow, someone else will.

- **Corruption Enables Crime**:
  The Purple Gang had the law in their pocket. They paid off coppers lookin' the other way while they smuggled booze. Today, software piracy thrives where the law is slack or bought off. Corruption is the grease that keeps the wheels of crime turnin'.
  Lesson: The fight against cybercrime ain't just technical. It's political. Strong, transparent laws and enforcement are just as important as firewalls and patches. Don't forget, the bad guys can work from places where the law doesn't care.

- **Adaptation is Crucial**:
  The Purple Gang was always one step ahead, switchin' up routes and tactics to avoid getting nabbed. Software pirates do the same, crackin' new security measures and stayin' ahead of the game. Adaptation is the name of the racket.
  Lesson: Cybersecurity is a moving target. You can't rely on one trick forever. Just like the gangsters had to stay ahead of the

law, your cybersecurity needs to keep up with new threats and tactics. Constant adaptation is survival.

- **End of One, Beginning of Another**:
  When Prohibition ended, the Purple Gang crumbled. But crime didn't stop, it just changed. Same with software piracy: shut down one racket, and another one springs up. There's always a new hustle waiting in the wings.
  Lesson: Just like the end of Prohibition didn't mean the end of crime, shutting down one form of cybercrime won't solve everything. Be prepared for new threats as old ones fade away. Always expect the next racket to pop up.

Cybersecurity Relevance: The Purple Gang ran the booze racket like kings. Today's hackers are doin' the same with software piracy—bootleggin' programs, sellin' 'em cheap, and runnin' off with the profits. Cybersecurity's lesson here is clear: piracy's not just a small-time operation; it's big business. If you don't lock down your intellectual property, some savvy crook will be sellin' it on the digital black market faster than you can say "Prohibition."

The Purple Gang's bootlegging operations and the phenomenon of software piracy are two sides of the same coin, separated only by time and technology. Both involve the illicit distribution of a valuable commodity, both require a network of distribution, and both show the lengths people will go to for financial gain.

Whether you're a gangster from the Prohibition era or a savvy individual navigating the digital age, the rules of the game remain the same. It's not personal; it's strictly business. And in any business, you've got to be smart, you've got to be prepared, and you've got to keep your eyes on the prize. Now, if you'll excuse me, I've got a high-stakes poker game to get to. Remember, the house always wins—unless you know how to play your cards right. Cheers!

Chapter 8: Keep Your Friends Close, But Your Enemies Closer

Let's dive deeper into that golden nugget of wisdom: "Keep your friends close, but your enemies closer." You might've heard it from that Corleone fella in "The Godfather," but let me tell ya, we've been living by that motto since before your grandpappy was in short pants.

See, in my line of work, you gotta keep tabs on everyone—your crew, the coppers, and especially those rival gangs. You think I got to where I am by turning a blind eye? Nah! I know what Johnny "The Snake" is up to on the South Side, and I keep tabs on what the O'Donnell crew is planning. Information, my friend, is the most valuable currency. I've got eyes and ears everywhere—bartenders, bellboys, even the paperboys. They're my informants, my little birds, whispering secrets into my ear.

Now, you might be wondering, how do I recruit these informants? Ah, it's a delicate dance, my friend. Sometimes it's through favors, sometimes through intimidation, and sometimes through good ol' cash. The key is to know what makes people tick. Once you've got that, you've got 'em in the palm of your hand.

In your world, these informants might be "threat intelligence feeds" or "security analysts." They're your eyes and ears in the digital realm, always on the lookout for the latest schemes and scams. You've got these hackers, phishers, and all sorts of cyber nogoodniks trying to bust into your vaults. If you don't know what they're up to, you're as good as broke, see? You've gotta study 'em, understand their tactics, their motivations, and maybe even infiltrate their forums and chat rooms. The more you know about your enemy, the better you can defend against 'em.

Just like I wouldn't trust any ol' Joe off the street, you shouldn't blindly trust any source of threat intelligence. Vet them, test the quality of their information, and only then integrate them into your security program. And remember, the best intelligence is timely, relevant, and actionable.

The Nuts and Bolts

- **Threat Intelligence Platforms:** These are your digital informants, constantly feeding you information about the latest threats. Platforms like Recorded Future or CrowdStrike offer real-time threat intelligence that you can integrate into your security systems.

- **Red Teaming and Blue Teaming:** Think of this as your training ground. These are good guys playing against one another to test your defenses and response measures. The Red Team tries to break in, and the Blue Team defends. It's like a scrimmage in the criminal world, a mock battle to prepare for the real war.

  - **Purple Teaming:** This is when the Red and Blue Teams work together to improve security. It's like when rival gangs form a truce to take down a common enemy.

- **Incident Response Plans:** These are your escape routes and safe houses. When things go south, and believe me, they will, you need to know exactly what to do to minimize the damage.

- **Tabletop Exercises:** These are like your strategy meetings, where you game out different scenarios and responses. In my world, we'd call this "planning the heist."

- **User Training**: Your crew is your first line of defense and your biggest vulnerability. Train them well. Run regular drills, send out fake phishing emails to see who bites, and always, always keep them on their toes.

The Gangster Wisdom: Lessons Learned

- **Never Underestimate Anyone:** Whether it's the shoeshine boy or the janitor, everyone has something valuable to offer. In cybersecurity, this means not overlooking "insignificant" threats that could be Trojan horses for bigger attacks.

- **Always Be Prepared:** I've got a hidden pocket for my cash, a concealed holster for my gun, and a secret compartment in my car. In your world, this means multi-factor authentication, encrypted communications, and regular backups.

- **Information is Power, But Timing is Everything:** Knowing about a rival's plan is good but knowing it in time to act is better. Real-time threat intelligence is crucial.

- **Trust, But Verify:** Double-crossing is an art in the gangster world, and in the digital world, impersonation is all too easy. Always double-check identities, whether it's a person or an email.

There you have it, my friends. A deep dive into the world of informants, intelligence, and the art of keeping your enemies closer than your pocketbook. Here are some real-world examples.

1. **The Las Vegas Fish Tank Breach - A Fishy Situation**

Ah, the tale of the Las Vegas Fish Tank Breach, see? It's one of those yarns that's so out there, you'd think it was cooked up by some wise guy in a smoky back room. But in the twisted world of cybersecurity, sometimes the facts are stranger than fiction. Let's take a plunge into how the old adage "Keep your friends close, but your enemies closer" fits into this wild caper.

In this gig, the hackers didn't muscle their way in through the usual joints like payment systems or employee records. Nah, these slick operators slipped in through a smart fish tank sitting pretty in the casino's lobby. You heard that right, pal—a fish tank hooked up to the internet was the Achilles' heel. (Schiffer, 2017)

Never Underestimate the Little Guy

In our line of work, it's always the little guy who throws you for a loop. Maybe it's the barkeep who catches a whisper of a big score, or the janitor who's got the keys to the whole joint. For this Las Vegas casino, the "little guy" was just a harmless fish tank, or so they thought.

The Art of Keeping an Eye on the Unusual Suspects

Just like any sharp gangster keeps tabs on everyone in his operation, from the top lieutenants to the lowly errand boys, a savvy cybersecurity strategy must account for all potential vulnerabilities, no matter how insignificant they may seem.

Let the fish tank breach be a wake-up call about the dangers of the Internet of Things (IoT). As more gadgets and gizmos get hooked up to the network, the potential for a hack job increases. The lesson here is to keep a close watch on all those connected devices, no matter how harmless they might look.

After a breach like this, any outfit with half a brain would start thinking about beefing up their IoT defenses. This could mean setting up network segmentation to keep the less secure devices in their own little corner, doing regular security check-ups on all connected gear, and keeping an eagle eye out for any funny business in real-time.

Lessons Learned:

- **Never Underestimate the Little Guy:** You'd think it was the high rollers or the vault that would get hit, right? Nah, these cyber goons slipped in through a *fish tank*. In our world, it's the small-time guys that end up bustin' your operation wide open. Even the smallest fish in the tank can cause a big splash if you ain't watchin'.
  Lesson: Don't ignore the small connected devices, especially the Internet of Things (IoT). They're easy to overlook, but they could open the door for hackers to waltz right into your systems. Stay sharp, and don't let these gadgets go unchecked.

- **Keep an Eye on the Unusual Suspects:** See, any smart boss keeps tabs on everyone in the operation, from the muscle down to the errand boys. Same goes for your network, pal. You might think that a flashy security system or a beefed-up firewall will do the trick, but if you ain't watching *everything*, even the oddballs like a fish tank, you're askin' for trouble.
  Lesson: Even the most insignificant device needs to be part of your security plan. Don't just focus on the big players like payment systems. Make sure you're keeping an eye on the smaller, connected gadgets, 'cause they're part of the crew too.

- Segment the Family Business: If you're running multiple operations, you never want them all tied together. You keep your booze racket separate from your gambling joints, so when one gets hit, the other stays clean. Same thing here—if one of your devices gets pinched, you don't want the whole network to go down like a house of cards.

Lesson: Network segmentation is your pal here. It's like keeping the different parts of your business separate. If your fish tank or smart light bulb gets hacked, you don't want the hackers crawling all the way to your sensitive data. Keep 'em locked in their own little box.

- **Watch for Funny Business in Real-Time:** A sharp boss can sniff out trouble before it hits. Same thing with cybersecurity—you gotta spot the odd stuff *while* it's happening. Don't wait until it's too late to see that something's wrong. You've always gotta be one step ahead of the troublemakers.
  Lesson: Use real-time monitoring tools to keep an eye on traffic. You see something fishy, like an internet-connected aquarium suddenly sending data to some shady part of the world? You act fast, nip it in the bud, and send those hackers swimming with the fishes.

Cybersecurity Relevance: Even the smallest crack in the operation can bring it all down. The Las Vegas Fish Tank breach? That's a perfect example of overlookin' the small fry. Hackers snuck in through a smart fish tank of all things, remindin' us that in cybersecurity, every connected device is a potential backdoor. You think it's just a harmless gadget, but if you ain't watchin' the details, you'll find your whole system floatin' belly up. Never underestimate the little guy.

So, whether you're running a high-stakes casino or a small online joint, remember this golden rule: "Keep your friends close, but your enemies closer." And always remember, in cybersecurity as in life, it ain't personal; it's strictly business. Cheers!

2. The Home Depot Breach - A Crack in the Foundation

The Home Depot Breach of 2014, a classic tale of what happens when you let your guard down. A story that drives home why the saying

"Keep your friends close, but your enemies closer" holds water in the world of cybersecurity just as much as in the gangster world. Let's hammer down the details, shall we?

Home Depot, a big shot in the home improvement retail game, found itself in hot water when hackers muscled their way into its payment systems. This breach exposed the credit card details of millions of customers. But here's the kicker: these hackers slipped in using a third-party vendor's credentials. (Stempel, 2020)

In our world, trust is more precious than gold. But even your most trusted associates can become your downfall if you're not careful. Home Depot trusted its third-party vendors, but that trust got exploited, leading to one of the biggest retail breaches in history.

The Art of Keeping All Players in Check

In the criminal underworld, you might trust your associates to handle different parts of the operation, but you'd always keep tabs on them. Home Depot's blunder was not keeping a closer eye on the security practices of its third-party vendors.

The Home Depot breach is a textbook example of why vendor risk management is crucial in cybersecurity. You might trust your vendors, but you also gotta verify their security measures and keep an eye on their activities.

The Art of Continuous Monitoring and Verification

After the breach, Home Depot took several steps to shore up its cybersecurity defenses, including better monitoring of vendors. They learned the hard way that it's not enough to trust; you gotta verify and keep a close watch on all the players involved in your network.

Lessons Learned:

- **Trust is a Double-Edged Sword**:
  In our world, trust is earned, but you always keep one eye open, just in case. Home Depot trusted its third-party vendors, and that's where it all went south. See, even the best associates can turn into your biggest headache if you're not keeping tabs on 'em. Hackers snuck in using the vendor's credentials, leaving Home Depot holdin' the bag.
  Lesson: Just 'cause you trust a vendor doesn't mean you take your hands off the wheel. You've got to keep a close watch on how your partners handle security, 'cause if they slip up, it's your operation that takes the hit.

- **Don't Let Your Guard Down**:
  In this breach, Home Depot let their guard down, and it cost them. You think you're secure, you get comfy, and boom—hackers are waltzing through the front door. Complacency is a killer in this line of work, and it's no different in the digital world.
  Lesson: Never get too comfortable with your security setup. Always be on guard, always be improving, and always be ready for an attack. The minute you think you're untouchable, that's when you get hit.

Cybersecurity Relevance: Home Depot let their guard down, see? In 2014, some hackers muscled their way in using a third-party vendor's access. This breach exposed millions of credit cards. The lesson here? In cybersecurity, trust is a dangerous game. You can't rely on your vendors without checkin' on 'em. Keep tabs on your partners just like you'd keep an eye on your crew, or you'll find your operation cracked wide open.

So, whether you're in the business of selling hammers or safeguarding data, remember this golden nugget of wisdom: "Keep your friends close, but your enemies closer." And let's not forget, in the realm of cybersecurity, it's never personal; it's strictly business. Cheers!

3. The Target Data Breach - Target's Achilles' Heel

Ah, the Target Data Breach of 2013, a classic tale of trust gone awry and a lesson in why you should always keep your friends close, but your enemies closer. Let's dive into the nitty-gritty of how this phrase applies to one of the most infamous cybersecurity incidents in recent history.

Target, a retail giant, found itself in the crosshairs when hackers gained access to its network, compromising the personal and financial information of millions of customers. But here's the kicker: the entry point wasn't some sophisticated hack into Target's main servers; it was through an HVAC vendor. That's right, a heating, ventilation, and air conditioning contractor! (Kassner, 2015)

Trust, But Verify

In the gangster world, you might trust a guy to do a job for you, but you'd always have someone keep an eye on him, just to make sure he doesn't double-cross you. Target trusted its HVAC vendor, a seemingly low-risk relationship, but failed to keep a close enough eye on the interactions between the vendor's systems and its own.

The Art of Keeping Peripheral Friends Under Scrutiny

In the underworld, even the smallest player can pose the biggest risk if overlooked. Target's HVAC vendor was a small player in the grand scheme of Target's operations, but the lack of scrutiny on this peripheral relationship led to a catastrophic breach.

Cybersecurity Relevance: The Target Methodology Post-Breach

After the breach, Target had to rethink its cybersecurity strategy, particularly concerning third-party vendors. The new approach involved stringent vetting processes and continuous monitoring of all third-party activities related to Target's systems. In essence, Target learned the hard way to keep its friends close but its "enemies" (potential vulnerabilities) even closer.

Post-breach, Target implemented robust vendor risk management protocols. These protocols included regular audits, real-time monitoring, and stringent compliance requirements, ensuring that all vendors—no matter how peripheral—were closely monitored.

Lessons Learned:

- **Trust, But Verify**:
  In our world, even if you trust a guy, you don't let him outta your sight. Target thought they could trust their HVAC vendor, but they didn't keep an eye on 'em. Next thing you know, the whole operation gets blown wide open, and millions of customer records are out in the wind.
  Lesson: Always keep tabs on your partners, no matter how small-time they look. Trust is nice, but verification? That's what keeps you outta hot water.

- **The Art of Vendor Risk Management**:
  Post-breach, Target wasn't gonna make the same mistake twice. They started running audits, making sure their vendors were up to snuff, and checking in on 'em regularly. It's like running a crew, you gotta know what everyone's up to and make sure they're playing by the rules.
  Lesson: Regular check-ins and strict protocols keep your operation safe. Don't leave anything to chance—'cause chance? That's for suckers.

Cybersecurity Relevance: Target learned the hard way that even the small players can bring down a giant. Hackers used an HVAC vendor's credentials to slip into their network, stealin' millions of credit card numbers. It's a reminder that in cybersecurity, the weakest link can ruin everything. Whether it's a vendor or a third-party system, you gotta scrutinize every connection to your network like you'd check for bugs in your joint.

So, whether you're a retail giant or a small business, remember this piece of gangster wisdom: "Keep your friends close, but your enemies closer." Cheers!

Got my eye on you (MidJourney, 2023)

4. Meyer Lansky's Intricate Web

Meyer Lansky, the "Mob's Accountant," a man who knew the value of a dollar and the cost of a life. He was a mastermind in organized crime, but what set him apart was his uncanny ability to navigate the treacherous waters of friendships and rivalries within the mob world.

Now, let's delve into how this phrase, "Keep your friends close, but your enemies closer," was practically Lansky's life motto.

Meyer Lansky was not just a financial genius; he was a social engineer of the highest order. He had connections everywhere, from the Italian Mafia to the Jewish mob, from politicians to law enforcement. He was friends with the likes of Lucky Luciano and Bugsy Siegel, but he also knew how to keep tabs on those who could pose a threat to him or his empire. (biography.com, 2021)

The Art of Keeping Enemies Closer

Lansky was a man who believed in insurance, not the kind you buy, but the kind you cultivate. He had dirt on everyone, from his closest allies to his fiercest competitors. This information was his insurance policy, ensuring that even his enemies thought twice before crossing him. He would often collaborate with rival factions or individuals, not out of friendship, but to keep a close eye on their activities.

Cybersecurity Relevance: The Lansky Method in the Digital Age

In the realm of cybersecurity, the Lansky Method would involve not just defending against known threats but actively engaging with the threat landscape. This could mean participating in hacker forums under an alias, or even hiring reformed hackers to understand the mindset and tactics of potential adversaries.

The Art of Digital Diplomacy

Just like Lansky would keep his enemies within arm's reach, a savvy cybersecurity expert might engage with the hacking community to understand the latest trends in malware, ransomware, and phishing attacks. This is not to say you become friends with the enemy, but rather that you understand them well enough to anticipate their moves.

Lessons Learned:

- **Information is Power:** Lansky held onto secrets like a safe full of cash. He knew who was doing what, and that gave him the leverage to control situations, making sure no one had the guts to cross him. It was how he survived in the cutthroat world of organized crime.
  Lesson: In the cyber world, data is your power. Know your vulnerabilities, know your enemies, and know your network better than anyone else. The more information you have, the better you can protect yourself from attacks. Stay ahead of the game by controlling the narrative, just like Lansky did.

- **Digital Diplomacy:** Just like Lansky played both sides to his benefit, a smart cybersecurity pro might hire reformed hackers or stay close to hacker communities. You don't get chummy with 'em, but you learn from them. You understand how they think, what tools they use, and how they operate. It's all about knowing what might be coming before it hits.
  Lesson: Engage with the hacker community, not as a friend, but as an observer. Know the latest trends in malware, ransomware, and phishing attacks so you can outsmart the crooks before they make a move. You don't have to like 'em, but understanding them could save your operation.

Cybersecurity Relevance: Meyer Lansky built his empire by keepin' a tight network of alliances. In cybersecurity, it's about the same...network segmentation. You gotta isolate parts of your system, so if one gets hit, the whole ship doesn't sink. Lansky's empire stretched far and wide, but each piece was fortified, just like how you need to keep your data separated and protected.

So, whether you're building a gambling empire or fortifying a digital fortress, remember the wisdom of Meyer Lansky: "Keep your friends close, but your enemies closer." And as always, it's never personal; it's strictly business. Cheers!

5. Lucky Luciano's Balancing Act

Charles "Lucky" Luciano, the godfather of modern organized crime in America and the brains behind the Five Families of New York. Now, there's a guy who truly grasped the essence of "Keep your friends close, but your enemies closer." Let's take a stroll down memory lane and see how Lucky played this timeless wisdom to his advantage in his life and criminal career. (Brown, n.d.)

Lucky was a visionary, seeing beyond the petty beefs and turf wars that plagued the underworld. He was the mastermind behind forming The Commission, a ruling body that brought various crime families together. But don't get it twisted, Lucky wasn't some naive peacemaker; he was a sharp operator who knew how to keep his pals in line and his enemies even closer.

The Art of Manipulating Enemies

Luciano had a real knack for turning enemies into allies, or at least into manageable threats. Take his relationship with Meyer Lansky, for example. They started off as rivals, but they became lifelong friends and business partners. But Lucky didn't just leave it at friendship; he made sure Lansky was involved in various ventures, effectively keeping him close and under his watchful eye.

Cybersecurity Relevance: The Lucky Method in Cybersecurity

In cybersecurity, the Lucky Method ain't just about building alliances for mutual gain but also for mutual surveillance. This means teaming up with other outfits on cybersecurity initiatives while keeping an eye on their moves to make sure they don't turn into threats themselves.

The Art of Cyber Alliances

Just like Lucky Luciano would form alliances to solidify his power, a sharp cybersecurity strategy might involve partnering up with other organizations, sharing threat intel, and working together on security protocols. But always keep a watchful eye on these allies. Make sure the shared info doesn't blow back on your own security and always double-check the intel you get.

Lessons Learned:

- **Strength in Unity, But Caution in Alliance:** Just like Lucky brought the Five Families together to solidify his control, cybersecurity pros should team up with other organizations to share threat intel and work on common security protocols. But like any sharp operator, you gotta watch your back. Even your allies could slip up or turn against you down the line.
  Lesson: Don't trust too easily. Stay sharp, keep your systems secure, and make sure the intel you share with others doesn't come back to haunt you. Just because you're working together doesn't mean they can't become your enemy later.

- **Know When to Cut Ties:** Luciano wasn't sentimental. When an alliance or friendship became a liability, he was quick to sever ties. In cybersecurity, this could mean ending a vendor relationship if their product becomes a security risk.
  Lesson: In cybersecurity, it's about working with other players in the field while watching their moves. You might be sharing threat intelligence, but keep tabs on who's getting access to your information. Make sure those partnerships don't end up biting you in the back.

Cybersecurity Relevance: Lucky Luciano was a master at playin' both sides, keepin' his enemies closer than his friends. That's what cybersecurity's all about, constant vigilance and balance. You don't just protect your systems; you monitor everything, includin' your allies. Luciano knew that to stay on top, he had to be smarter than the rest. Same goes for you. Always know who's got access, and never trust anyone too much.

So, whether you're orchestrating the criminal underworld or navigating the complex maze of cybersecurity, take a page out of Lucky Luciano's book: "Keep your friends close, but your enemies closer." Cheers!

Chapter 9: Don't Let Anyone Know What You're Thinking

Ah, kid, let me tell ya a thing or two about the streets of 1930s. The city was alive with the hum of cars, the chatter of speakeasies, and the ever-present danger that lurked in its shadows. In my line of work, one rule kept me alive: "Don't let anyone know what you're thinking." It was the golden rule, a mantra of survival. But who would've thought that this old gangster wisdom would be the key to navigating the digital age?

The Streets of New York and the Digital Alleyways

Back in the day, if you wore your heart on your sleeve, you'd find yourself at the bottom of the Hudson. Whether you were planning a heist, setting up a rival, or just trying to keep your territory intact, secrecy was your best friend. The moment someone got wind of your plans, you were as good as dead.

Fast forward to today's digital age, and the streets have transformed into virtual alleyways. But the game? Oh, it's still the same. In the world of cybersecurity, if you let your guard down and reveal your defense strategies, you're inviting trouble. Just like the old days, the moment your rivals know what you're up to, you're done for.

Examples from the Alleyways of Cybersecurity

- **The Hidden Vault:** Imagine you've got a vault, see? And in this vault, you've got all the secrets, your plans, your contacts, everything. Now, if you go blabbing about where this vault is or how to access it, you're asking for trouble. In the digital world, this vault is your database. Companies that openly discuss their security measures or boast about their impenetrable defenses often find themselves as prime targets for hackers. Why? Because they've shown their hand.

- **The Double-Cross:** Remember Tommy "Two-Times"? He was always thinking he was one step ahead, but the moment he spilled the beans about his next job, he was set up. In the digital realm, insider threats are a real concern. Employees, if turned or coerced, can reveal sensitive information. It's essential to keep security protocols confidential and limit knowledge to only those who need to know.

- **The Speakeasy Password:** Back in the Prohibition days, you couldn't just waltz into a speakeasy without the password. It was a secret, whispered among trusted folks. Similarly, encryption keys and passwords in the digital world should be kept hush-hush. The moment they're out in the open, your data is as exposed as a mobster in a police lineup.

- **The Modern-Day Moll and Her Secrets:** Let's talk about Sally "Silent" Malone. She was the best moll in the business, not because she was the prettiest or the wittiest, but because she knew how to keep her mouth shut. In today's world, Sally would be the equivalent of a top-notch encryption algorithm. She takes information, locks it up tight, and doesn't let anyone in on the secret. Only those with the right key (or in Sally's case, the right charm) can get the information they need.

Here's a few real examples for ya.

145

1. The Apple-FBI Tango

Lemme take you back to a time not so long ago, but worlds apart from the smoky speakeasies and Tommy guns of my day. It's 2016, see, and the whole world's in a tizzy over this Apple vs. FBI hullabaloo. But if you squint just right, it's like watching a high-stakes poker game in one of those back rooms I used to frequent.

So, the G-men, the Feds, the FBI, they're all hot on the trail of some real bad eggs responsible for a terrible act in San Bernardino. They get their mitts on one of the shooter's fancy Apple telephones, but there's a catch - they can't get in. It's locked up tighter than a speakeasy on a Sunday morning.

The Feds, they go knockin' on Apple's door, askin' real nice-like for a way in. They want Apple to whip up a special key, a backdoor, to get past the phone's defenses. But Apple, they ain't no chump. They know the score. They've built their empire on trust, on the promise that what you put on their gadgets stays private. It's their bread and butter, see?

Apple's head honcho, a slick fella by the name of Tim Cook, he channels his inner gangster and essentially tells the Feds, "You might wear the badges, but you ain't gettin' our secrets." It's like when Big Joey Marconi used to say, "Don't let anyone know what you're thinking." Apple's thinking? Their encryption, their secret sauce. Give that away, and they're just another player in the game, not the kingpin. (Kharpal, 2016)

By refusing the Feds, Apple's sending a message loud and clear: their user's privacy, that's sacred. It's not just about one phone or one case. If they spill the beans, if they let the Feds know their "thinking," who's to say where it stops? Today it's one phone, tomorrow it's a million. It's like giving away the combination to your safe. Once it's out there, anyone can waltz right in.

The Feds, they eventually find another way in, without Apple's help. But the message was sent. Apple showed the world that they're not just in it for the dough. They've got principles, see? And in this crazy, mixed-up digital age, that counts for a lot.

Lessons Learned:

- **Don't Expose Your Secrets**:
  Apple understood that creating a backdoor for one phone could set a dangerous precedent, potentially opening the door for future demands and weakening their overall security.
  Lesson: Keep your proprietary methods and secrets protected. Once you give them away, you may lose control over how they are used in the future.

- **Controlled Information is Power**:
  By refusing to provide the backdoor, Apple controlled the narrative and maintained its position as a protector of user privacy. They demonstrated that not revealing their "thinking" can keep them in a position of strength.
  Lesson: In negotiations, retaining control of information is a source of power. Don't reveal everything too soon; strategic withholding of information can give you an advantage.

- **Keep Your Cards Close**:
  Tim Cook's refusal to create a backdoor aligned with the principle of not showing your hand too early. Apple kept its encryption methods secret, preventing broader access to their technology.
  Lesson: In business and negotiations, it's often better to keep your strategies, methods, or plans closely guarded until it's absolutely necessary to reveal them. Transparency has its place, but timing and discretion are key.

Cybersecurity Relevance: Picture this: Apple's holdin' their cards close, refusin' to crack open a locked iPhone for the Feds. It's a classic standoff. Just like in the old mob days, you don't give away your trade secrets, even if it means dodgin' the law. This case set the tone for privacy and encryption in the digital world. It's about standin' your ground when everyone's after your gold, keepin' that back door shut no matter who's knockin'. Privacy, in the digital age, is a treasure, and Apple? They weren't gonna let anyone crack the vault.

So, kiddo, next time you're in a bind, remember the Apple-FBI dance. Sometimes, the smartest play is to keep your cards close to your vest and not let anyone know what you're thinking. After all, in the words of Big Joey, "In this game, trust is more valuable than gold." And Apple? They've got trust in spades.

2. The Shadow Brokers Racket (2016)

Alright, listen up. There's this gang, goes by the name of the Shadow Brokers. Sounds like a name straight outta those pulp magazines, don't it? Now, in the hot summer of '16, these wise guys start making noise, claiming they've pinched some real top-shelf tools from the bigwigs at the NSA. Rumor has it, these tools were the handiwork of the Equation Group, which some say is just a fancy name for the NSA's backroom boys.

These Brokers, they ain't just blowing smoke. They spill a bit of their stash for the world to see, and suddenly, everyone's talking. Among the treasures is this little number called "EternalBlue." Fancy moniker, right? Well, it's the master key to a lot of locked doors, if you catch my drift. And before you know it, it's being used in this grand heist dubbed WannaCry in '17. (cyberlaw.ccdcoe.org, 2016)

The Fallout:

- **Global Pandemonium:** This WannaCry operation? It's the real deal. Hits places in over 150 countries. We're talking hospitals, businesses, train stations. Everything's in a tizzy. Folks can't access their stuff unless they cough up some dough.

- **The Blame Game:** The NSA's got egg on their face. People are up in arms, thinking, "You got these master keys and you ain't telling the locksmiths or the folks?"

- **The Price Tag:** This ain't small potatoes. The damage? It's in the billions. All from this one caper.

Lessons Learned:

- **Even Top Security Can Be Breached:** The Shadow Brokers managed to steal top-secret tools from the NSA's Equation Group, showing that even the most secure organizations can have vulnerabilities.
  Lesson: No system is invincible. Always assume your defenses can be breached, and have contingency plans in place for when they are.

- **Failure to Share Crucial Information Can Lead to Greater Damage:** The NSA knew about EternalBlue's vulnerabilities but didn't inform software vendors or the public until it was too late. This delay allowed malicious actors to exploit the tool.
  Lesson: Transparency and proactive communication are key. When a vulnerability is discovered, informing relevant parties quickly can prevent wide-scale damage.

- **Global Consequences of Cybersecurity Lapses:** The WannaCry attack affected over 150 countries, bringing down hospitals, businesses, and essential services worldwide, all because of a single cybersecurity lapse.
  Lesson: Cybersecurity is a global concern. A single breach can have far-reaching consequences, highlighting the need for international collaboration in defending against cyber threats.

Cybersecurity Relevance: These Shadow Brokers? They remind me of those old-time informants, sellin' out to the highest bidder. Only instead of secrets from the street, they're peddlin' cyber weapons. They got their hands on NSA's prized tools and leaked 'em, makin' hackers everywhere drool. In cybersecurity, control of your weapons—your exploits—is everything. When you lose that control, it's like lettin' a rival gang get their hands on your best muscle. That EternalBlue hack? It was the cyber equivalent of a Tommy gun sprayin' the whole world.

This whole mess with the Shadow Brokers? It's a textbook case of "Don't Let Anyone Know What You're Thinking." The suits at the NSA, they had their little secrets, their game plans. But once those got out in the open? It was bedlam. It's a lesson for all of us, from the speakeasies to the cyber highways: always play your cards close, but also make sure you're playing with a full deck.

3. The Sony Pictures Shakedown (2014)

Gather 'round, folks. Let me spin you a yarn about Tinseltown, where the glitz and glamour ain't all it's cracked up to be. So, there's this big-shot movie studio, Sony Pictures Entertainment. They're in the business of making those silver screen dreams. But in 2014, they found themselves in a real-life noir thriller.

Outta nowhere, these shadowy figures, calling themselves the "Guardians of Peace" (sounds like a dime novel title, right?), pull off a heist like no other. They break into Sony's vaults, but they ain't after gold or jewels. They're after the real treasure in the modern age: information. And boy, do they hit the jackpot. Everything from personal dirt on the big stars to those flicks that ain't even hit the theaters yet, they grab it all. (Peterson, 2014)

The Spoils:

- **The Gossip Columns' Dream:** Personal emails between the big players at Sony, filled with juicy tidbits, the kind that'd make any tabloid reporter salivate.
- **The Unseen Films:** Movies, some of 'em not even released yet, are snatched up and thrown into the wild, free for anyone with an internet connection.
- **The Nitty-Gritty:** Financial records, employee details, and strategic plans – the kind of stuff that keeps the big bosses up at night.

But these wise guys, they ain't content with just the loot. They wanna send a message, see? They start plastering Sony's own billboards with their calling cards, taunting 'em, showing off just how deep they got into the studio's business. It's like they strolled into the joint, took what they wanted, and then danced on the tables on their way out.

The Fallout:

- **The Big Reveal:** The whole world's watching as these goons start spilling Sony's secrets. We're talking scripts, salaries, and even some spicy emails between the bigwigs. It's a PR nightmare.
- **The Blame Game:** Fingers are pointed every which way. Some say it's an inside job, others reckon it's those North Korean fellas getting all riled up about a comedy flick Sony's putting out. The plot's thicker than Chicago fog.
- **The Dollar Damage:** Beyond the stolen data, Sony's gotta shell out big bucks to clean up the mess. Legal fees, PR stunts, and not to mention the moolah lost from those leaked films.

Lessons Learned:

- **Public Relations Can Suffer Just as Much as Security:** The leaked personal emails and internal documents embarrassed Sony, damaging relationships with stars, producers, and the media.

Lesson: A breach can harm your company's reputation as much as, or more than, financial loss. Preventative measures and damage control strategies need to be in place to handle the fallout.

- **Hackers Can Weaponize Public Exposure:**
  The "Guardians of Peace" didn't just steal data; they publicly humiliated Sony by releasing it for all to see, undermining their authority and credibility.
  Lesson: Cybercriminals don't just steal; they can destroy. A robust cybersecurity plan needs to include strategies to mitigate the effects of public exposure.

Cybersecurity Relevance: Ah, Sony, they got shook down worse than a corner store durin' a protection racket. Hackers bust into their vault and grabbed all the juicy stuff: unreleased films, gossip-filled emails, you name it. It's a lesson straight from the streets: guard your most valuable goods, or someone else will use 'em against you. Sony thought they were too big to fail, but a well-planned digital shakedown put 'em in their place. In cybersecurity, even the big dogs gotta watch their backs.

This Sony caper? It's a stark reminder of "Don't Let Anyone Know What You're Thinking." The moment you let your guard down, thinking you're safe in your ivory tower, that's when they get ya. In the glitzy world of Hollywood or the smoky backrooms of our joints, the rules are the same: always play it close to the vest.

4. The Ashley Madison Debacle (2015)

Alright, pull up a chair, and let me paint you a picture of the digital age, a time when secrets weren't whispered in dimly lit alleyways but typed behind glowing screens. The year was 2015, and the joint everyone was whispering about was Ashley Madison. This wasn't your run-of-the-mill gin joint; it was an exclusive club for folks looking to step out on their better halves. But, as any wise guy knows, the bigger the operation, the bigger the target on its back.

Ashley Madison, with its snazzy tagline "Life is short. Have an affair," was raking in the moolah, promising discretion to its clientele. But every empire has its enemies, and this digital haven was no exception. Some cyber hoodlums, not fans of the establishment's dealings, decided it was time for a shakedown. (Krebs, 2022)

The Heist:

- **The Digital Vault:** This wasn't about swiping a few bucks from the till. These wise guys were after the crown jewels: the user database. We're talking names, addresses, even those hush-hush fantasies folks whispered about.

- **The Big Reveal:** Once they had their mitts on the goods, they didn't just sit on it. No, they began leaking the names, turning up the heat bit by bit. From your everyday Joe to the bigwigs, no one was safe.

The Aftermath:

- **Trust in Tatters:** Ashley Madison, once the talk of the town, found itself in the gutter. Its clientele, once loyal, scattered like rats from a sinking ship.

- **The Real Cost:** Sure, there were lawsuits, settlements, and all that jazz. But the real damage? The homes torn apart, careers derailed, and the dark cloud that hung over those named and shamed.

- **The Manhunt:** The coppers, they were on the prowl, trying to nab these digital gangsters. But the real story wasn't about catching the culprits; it was about the fragility of trust in the digital age.

Who wants to be my friend? (Midjourney, 2023)

Here's where the rubber meets the road, kid. Whether you're operating in the Prohibition-era streets or the vast expanse of the internet, the game remains the same. The phrase "Don't Let Anyone Know What You're Thinking" ain't just some catchy line; it's the lifeblood of any operation. Because the moment you think you're untouchable, that's when they come knocking. And in this world, where secrets are currency, you best believe there's always someone looking to make a withdrawal.

Lessons Learned:

- **No Operation is 100% Secure:** Ashley Madison promised discretion to its users, guaranteeing their secrets would remain locked away. But once hackers targeted their "digital vault" containing sensitive user data, the illusion of security was shattered.
  Lesson: No matter how secure you think your systems are, you're always a target. Never assume you're untouchable, and always keep improving your defenses.

- **The Bigger the Target, the Bigger the Risk:** Ashley Madison's business model relied on the promise of privacy for millions of users engaging in discreet affairs, making it a highly attractive target for cyber attackers.
  Lesson: If your business deals with sensitive information, especially on a large scale, you're a prime target for cybercriminals. Ensure your security measures reflect the magnitude of the data you're responsible for.

- **Trust is Fragile in the Digital Age:** After the breach, Ashley Madison's clients fled, and the company's reputation never recovered. The breach wasn't just about lost data—it was about broken trust.
  Lesson: In the digital world, trust is the currency that keeps businesses running. Once that trust is broken, it's nearly impossible to regain, and customers will quickly jump ship.

- **Hackers Don't Just Steal, They Expose:** These cybercriminals weren't just after financial gain. They wanted to publicly expose Ashley Madison's users and humiliate them, proving that sometimes the motive goes beyond money.
  Lesson: Hackers' goals aren't always financial. Sometimes they aim for maximum public exposure and humiliation, making it essential to treat security breaches as more than just a business risk.

- **Secrets are Dangerous in the Wrong Hands:** When personal information about affairs and fantasies was leaked, it became clear that secrets can be as valuable as any financial asset and more devastating when exposed.
  Lesson: In today's world, personal and sensitive information is as valuable as money. Protecting it should be a top priority because its exposure can have life-altering consequences for those involved.

Cybersecurity Relevance: Ashley Madison thought they could keep their dirty little secrets safe, but every operation's got its weak spots. Hackers broke in, exposin' user details and wreakin' havoc on lives like a botched heist. The lesson here? Trust is fragile, and once broken, it's near impossible to fix. In cybersecurity, it's not just about protectin' data—it's about protectin' reputations. You lose one, you might as well be packin' it in, 'cause your business is finished.

Alright, kid, gather 'round. Let me tell ya about a little get-together that went south real fast. It's a tale that'll teach ya why you should always keep your cards close to your vest.

5. The Apalachin Meeting (1957)

So, picture this: It's the late '50s, and the big bosses of the underworld decide they need a little pow-wow. A sit-down, if you will. The place? A quiet, out-of-the-way joint in Apalachin, New York, owned by a fella named Joe "The Barber" Barbara. Now, Joe, he's a made man, a capo in the Bufalino family. He's got this sprawling estate, perfect for a discreet meeting of the minds.

Fancy seeing you here? (Midjourney, 2023)

The idea was simple: get all the big players from across the country under one roof, hash out some disagreements, and maybe carve up some territories. We're talking about over 60 of the most powerful men in the underworld. The who's who of the Mafia.

Now, here's where things got dicey. These wise guys, they rolled into town in flashy cars, wearing their finest threads. They might've been trying to keep the meeting hush-hush, but they sure weren't subtle about their arrival. And in a small town like Apalachin? Well, let's just say it raised a few eyebrows.

Local law enforcement got wind of this unusual gathering. And when they started seeing license plates from all over the country, they knew something was up. Before you knew it, the place was swarming with cops, and our discreet little meeting turned into one of the biggest roundups of mobsters in history.

See, the mistake these fellas made was thinking they could flaunt their presence without consequences. They underestimated the power of discretion. Instead of arriving quietly, they paraded into town like they owned the joint. They might've been thinking big, but they sure weren't thinking smart. (PETERS, 2013)

Lessons Learned:

- **Always Be Discreet**: The mob bosses arrived in flashy cars and fine suits, drawing unnecessary attention to what was supposed to be a low-key meeting. Their over-the-top arrival signaled trouble, making it easy for law enforcement to spot them.
  Lesson: If you're trying to keep something quiet, don't flaunt it. Subtlety and discretion are key to keeping operations under the radar.

- **Know Your Surroundings**:
  Apalachin, New York, was a small town where outsiders naturally raised suspicion. The mob bosses forgot that in a small community, strangers, especially in large numbers, stand out.
  Lesson: Always consider the environment you're operating in. What works in a big city may not fly in a small town where people notice unusual activity.

Cybersecurity Relevance: The Apalachin Meeting? It was supposed to be hush-hush, a quiet pow-wow between the biggest names in the mob. But one slip-up, and the Feds were all over it. This is a textbook lesson for cybersecurity: don't let your plans slip out. Just like the mob bosses who had their secrets exposed, a security breach can leave your whole operation in ruins. Keep your network secure, 'cause one careless leak, and it's game over.

The Apalachin Meeting is a classic example of why you should never let anyone know what you're thinking. In the world of wise guys and gangsters, one slip, one moment of carelessness, can cost you everything. Remember that.

Alright, kid, let me paint a clearer picture for ya. The Valachi incident wasn't just a hiccup; it was a seismic shift in the underworld. Grab a drink, light up a cigar, and let me take you on a trip down memory lane.

6. Joe Valachi Breaks Omertà (1963)

Joe Valachi, a foot soldier, was part of the Genovese family, one of the Five Families that ran New York's underworld. He wasn't the sharpest tool in the shed, but he was loyal, did his jobs, and kept his mouth shut. That's what made his eventual betrayal so shocking. (Henry, 2023)

The Prison Drama:

By the early '60s, Valachi's behind bars, and the walls start talking. Whispers float around that Vito Genovese, the big boss himself, has put a price on Joe's head. Now, whether that was true or just prison chatter, we'll never really know. But Joe believed it. And in our world, perception's as good as reality.

One day, Joe spots a guy he thinks is there to whack him. In a panic, he jumps the guy and kills him. Only problem? Wrong guy. Joe's just added to his problems.

The Betrayal:

Now, the Feds had been trying to crack the Mafia code for years. They'd heard the rumors, the tales of a secret society with its own language, rituals, and hierarchy. But it was like chasing a ghost. Enter Joe Valachi, scared and looking for protection. He sees an out and takes it, becoming the government's golden goose.

The Mafia's power wasn't just in its muscle; it was in its mystery. Outsiders never knew how it operated, who was in charge, or what they were planning. That secrecy kept them safe. But with Valachi's testimony, the veil was lifted.

- **The Power of Omertà:** This code of silence was the Mafia's armor. It wasn't just about not ratting; it was about not revealing the inner workings, the family secrets. Valachi tore that armor apart.

- **The Domino Effect:** After Valachi came forward, others followed. The floodgates opened, leading to more informants, more arrests, and more convictions.

Lessons Learned:

- **Perception Becomes Reality**: Valachi's belief that Vito Genovese had put a hit on him—whether true or not—led him to act irrationally, killing the wrong person in panic. **Lesson**: In cybersecurity, if your crew *thinks* there's a breach or threat but don't confirm it, they'll overreact, which could lead to a bigger mess. Or worse, if they assume all's well without double-checking, you'll get burned when something slips through. You gotta manage the perception and keep your people sharp.

- **The Power of One Informant**: Valachi's betrayal had a domino effect, leading to more informants, more arrests, and significant damage to the Mafia. His testimony broke open years of secrecy.

Lesson: One breach can lead to a flood. You get one hacker inside, and he'll open the door for his pals. That's why you need layers of security, constant monitoring, and quick incident response. Don't let one crack turn into a sinkhole.

- **Fear Leads to Desperation**: Valachi turned against his own out of fear for his life. His desperate actions came from feeling cornered.
  Lesson: Same goes for your digital world. If a hacker or insider gets desperate, they're gonna get sloppy. They'll leave tracks or try to cover their trail in a way that raises flags. Use that to your advantage, monitor for odd behavior, and when things start lookin' fishy, clamp down fast before they can bolt.

Cybersecurity Relevance: Joe Valachi broke the code of silence, spillin' the Mafia's secrets to the Feds. In the world of cybersecurity, insiders are just as dangerous. When someone on the inside flips, all your well-guarded data could be laid bare. This ain't just a story about loyalty, it's a cautionary tale about insider threats. You gotta watch everyone, even your most trusted soldiers, 'cause if they talk, your whole empire could crumble.

The Valachi saga is a warning for all of us. In our world, and in yours, always guard your secrets, trust carefully, and remember: sometimes, what you don't say is more powerful than what you do.

The world may have changed, with its fancy gadgets and its worldwide webs, but the rules? They're still the same. Whether you're navigating the grimy streets of 1930's New York or the vast expanse of the internet, remember: "Don't let anyone know what you're thinking." Keep your cards close to your chest, and you might just come out on top.

Chapter 10: Never Sell What You Love

The glitz and glamour of the 1930s! The jazz, the flappers, and the ever-present allure of the forbidden. But amidst the speakeasies and the Tommy guns, there were lessons to be learned, lessons that resonate even in today's digital age. Paul Cicero, a wise guy from the old neighborhood, once told me, "The first rule of business is never sell something you love." At the time, I thought he was talking about his prized Cadillac or maybe that gold watch he always wore. But as the years went by, I realized he was talking about something far more profound.

In the gangster world, selling something you love could mean betraying a trusted friend or giving up control of a lucrative racket. It meant compromising your core values for a quick buck. In today's world of cybersecurity, the principle remains the same. It's about not compromising on essential security measures or core values for short-term gains or conveniences.

The Temptation of Convenience Over Security:

- **The Scenario:** Many companies, in a bid to make user experiences smoother, might opt for simpler authentication processes, skipping multi-factor authentication or other security measures.

- **The Point:** By prioritizing convenience over security, these companies are essentially "selling" their commitment to user safety. And when a breach happens, the trust they've built over years can evaporate overnight.

The Allure of Fast Deployment:

- **The Scenario:** In the race to be the first to market, some software developers might push their products out without thorough security testing.

- **Lessons Learned:** Launching a product without ensuring its security is akin to selling your reputation. Once hackers find and exploit vulnerabilities, the damage to the company's reputation and user trust can be irreversible.

Data Monetization and Privacy:

- **The Scenario:** Some companies, hungry for additional revenue streams, might sell user data to advertisers without explicit consent.

- **The Point:** By trading user privacy for revenue, companies are selling their integrity. In the age of data breaches and increasing concerns over privacy, such actions can lead to significant backlash and legal repercussions.

Short-Term Gains Over Long-Term Security:

- **The Scenario:** To cut costs, a company might opt for cheaper, less secure infrastructure or might not invest in ongoing cybersecurity training for its employees.

- **The Point:** By prioritizing short-term financial gains over long-term security, companies are selling their future. A single major cyberattack can cost far more than what was saved, both in terms of money and reputation.

Meeting of the minds (Midjourney, 2023)

In the smoky backrooms of speakeasies, deals were made, and alliances were formed. But the wise guys knew that some things were sacred. In the realm of cybersecurity, the same principle applies. Whether it's user trust, data integrity, or the very reputation of a business, some things are too precious to be compromised.

1. Panama Papers Leak (2016)

Alright, gather 'round, see, 'cause I'm about to spill the beans on a tale that's got more twists and turns than a back alley in Brooklyn. We're talkin' about the Panama Papers Leak of 2016, a real doozy that shook the world to its core and left a trail of destruction in its wake. So, sit tight and listen up, 'cause this story's got lessons for all of us wise guys in the business.

The Setup:

So, we got this high-falutin' law firm, Mossack Fonseca, nestled in the heart of Panama, dealin' with the big fish, the kinda clients with deep pockets and deeper secrets. They're sittin' on a treasure trove of sensitive data, the sort that can make kings and topple empires. But here's where they slip – they're skimpin' on the security, leavin' the vault door wide open for any street rat with the guts to sneak in. (Harding, 2016)

The Heist:

Then, outta nowhere, the storm hits. We're talkin' about a leak of epic proportions – 11.5 million documents exposed for the world to see! It's like the floodgates opened, and out poured the dirty laundry of politicians, celebrities, and high-rollers from every corner of the globe. The air's thick with scandal, and the world's watchin' as the mighty fall.

The Fallout:

Now, Mossack Fonseca, they're in a real jam. The jig is up, and the world knows they've been playin' a dangerous game. The trust is broken, the reputation's tarnished, and it ain't long before the firm's lights go out for good. It's a one-way ticket to Palookaville, all 'cause they traded what they should've cherished, integrity and the safety of their client's secrets.

Lessons Learned:

- **Secrets Always Find a Way Out:** The leak exposed 11.5 million documents, revealing the private dealings of politicians, celebrities, and the wealthy. What was supposed to remain secret was laid bare for the world to see.
  Lesson: In a world where information flows easily, secrets are hard to keep. The best way to avoid scandal or exposure is to operate with transparency and integrity from the start.

- **Reputation is Priceless:** Once the leak happened, Mossack Fonseca's reputation was irreparably damaged, leading to the firm's eventual closure. Trust was shattered, and there was no way to recover.
  Lesson: Reputation is hard to build but easy to destroy. Guard your reputation with everything you've got, because once it's lost, it's almost impossible to get back.

- **Cherish What's Valuable:** Mossack Fonseca failed to protect what should have been their most prized possession: the trust and confidentiality of their clients. By losing sight of this, they lost everything.
  Lesson: Never sell out what's truly valuable—whether it's your integrity, trust, or relationships. Protect what matters most at all costs.

Cybersecurity Relevance: Panama Papers was like someone crackin' open the boss's safe and lettin' all the dirty laundry fly. A little carelessness, and boom, 11.5 million documents out in the open. In the cyber world, that's what happens when you don't lock down your system tight. This leak wasn't just about cash, it was about trust, loyalty, and reputation. You mess up, and you're takin' down not just yourself but everyone else who's bettin' on you. Cybersecurity is about protectin' the secrets, 'cause once they're out, there ain't no goin' back.

Whether you're runnin' booze during Prohibition or guardin' the secrets of the world's elite, you gotta have principles. You gotta safeguard what's entrusted to ya, and never, I mean never, trade your core values for a quick buck. Mossack Fonseca, they thought they could dance with the devil and walk away unscathed, but they ended up playin' a losing hand.

In this game, whether you're navigatin' the shadowy corners of the underworld or the intricate web of the digital age, loyalty and integrity are your best pals. Compromise 'em, and you're settin' yourself up for a fall. So, remember, kid, stick to your guns, protect what you love, and don't let the allure of easy money lead ya down the path of ruin. 'Cause once you sell out, there ain't no comin' back, and all that's left is the echo of what could've been.

2. Uber Data Breach & Cover-Up (2016)

I got another tale from good 'ole 2016. The city was abuzz with whispers and the shadows were tellin' tales of a heist pulled off by the big shots at Uber. Yeah, you heard me right, the high and mighty ride-hailin' joint that thought they were too clever for the rest of us. (apnews.com, 2023)

The Lay of the Land:

So, here's how it all went down. Uber, the kingpin of the ride-hailin' world, sittin' on a throne of gold, thinkin' they're untouchable. But, you see, every empire's got its secrets, and Uber was no different. They were guardin' 'em like a lion with a fresh kill. But, as fate would have it, they let their guard down, and bam! They're starin' down the barrel of a data breach – we're talkin' data of 57 million users and drivers floatin' in the wind.

The Underhanded Deal:

Now, any wise guy with half a brain would know, when you find yourself in hot water, you gotta face the music. But Uber, they had other plans. They decided to play a dangerous game, thinkin' they could make the whole mess disappear. They cough up a hefty $100,000 to the wise guys who pulled off the breach, tellin' 'em to zip it and make the stolen data vanish. It's a classic cover-up, a high-stakes gamble to keep the law and the public blind to their shenanigans.

The House of Cards Tumbles:

But, as the old sayin' goes, what's done in the dark will come to light. The truth, it's got a knack for diggin' its way out, and when it does, it's like a tidal wave. Uber's dirty deeds are laid bare for the world to see, and let me tell ya, the fallout is nothin' short of a spectacle. They're hit with lawsuits left and right, fines through the roof, and their once-gleamin' reputation is dragged through the gutter. The big cheeses at the helm take a fall, and what's left of Uber is scramblin' to pick up the pieces.

Your car is here. (Midjourney, 2023)

The Street Wisdom:

So, here's the kicker, kid. Uber, they were sittin' pretty, but they let greed cloud their judgment, traded their core values for a shot at dodgin' the bullet. They pawned off what should've been sacred – the trust of the people and the integrity of their name. And what did they get in return? A one-way ticket to Palookaville.

Lessons Learned:

- **The Truth Will Always Come Out**: Despite Uber's efforts to hide the breach, the truth eventually surfaced, causing massive damage to the company's reputation and leading to

lawsuits and fines.
Lesson: No matter how well you think you can hide the truth, it will eventually come out. Transparency and honesty are critical to maintaining trust and long-term success.

- **Short-Term Solutions Lead to Long-Term Consequences**: Uber's decision to pay off the hackers in secret seemed like a quick fix, but it resulted in long-term damage to their brand, significant legal consequences, and the loss of top executives.
  Lesson: Short-term fixes or cover-ups may seem tempting, but they often lead to much greater long-term problems. It's better to address the issue properly from the start.

- **Transparency is Key to Maintaining Trust**: Uber's failure to be transparent about the data breach eroded trust with its users and drivers, creating a backlash that damaged its credibility.
  Lesson: Transparency is essential to maintaining trust. If something goes wrong, be open and honest with your stakeholders to preserve your reputation and integrity.

Cybersecurity Relevance: Uber, they tried to play it slick. Hush money, a quick payoff, but in this game, the truth always finds a way out. They paid to keep their mouths shut, but the fallout was brutal. In the world of cyber, cover-ups don't stay buried. You gotta face the music and protect what matters most, transparency and trust. Uber lost big, not just on the breach but on their reputation. In cybersecurity, hiding the mess don't clean it up, it just makes the stink worse.

In this game, whether you're runnin' the back alleys or sittin' atop a tech empire, your word is gold. You tarnish it, and you're no better than a two-timin' rat. So, engrave this in your noggin, never pawn off what you hold dear, 'cause once it's gone, all the dough in the world ain't gonna bring it back. Stay true to your code, play the game straight, and let fate do its dance. That's the creed of the underworld, and it rings true whether you're dodgin' bullets or navigatin' the digital maze.

3. RSA Security Breach (2011)

Gather 'round, folks, 'cause I'm about to lay down a tale that's as twisty as the streets of old Chicago. We're diving deep into the RSA Security Breach of 2011 – a real doozy that had the cyber joint rattlin' and the big shots in a tizzy.

The Setup:

So, here's the lowdown. RSA was the top dog in the security game, the real McCoy, holdin' the keys to countless digital kingdoms with their fancy SecurID tokens. These gadgets were the cat's pajamas, designed to keep the riffraff out and the secrets under lock and key. But, as fate would have it, RSA got a little too cozy, a little too sure of themselves.

The Heist:

Like a bolt from the blue, a gang of cyber hoods pulled off a heist for the ages, crackin' RSA's safe and swipin' the crown jewels, critical information related to them SecurID tokens. It was a slap in the face, see? The very treasure RSA cherished and vowed to safeguard was now in the clutches of the underworld.

The Fallout:

The grapevine was buzzin', and the news hit the streets – RSA, the once invincible titan, had been taken for a ride. Trust in their security solutions took a nosedive, and clients were givin' 'em the hairy eyeball, wonderin' if their secrets were still in Fort Knox. RSA found themselves in hot water, scramblin' to mend fences and win back the trust they'd squandered. (GREENBERG, 2021)

Lessons Learned:

- **Protect What You Hold Dear**: RSA's core value was securing their clients' digital assets through their SecurID tokens, but they failed to fully safeguard the system that was meant to protect others.
  Lesson: When your business is based on protecting something valuable, that becomes your sacred duty. Never compromise or let your guard down on what's most important.

- **Transparency in Crisis is Key**: RSA scrambled to address the breach and regain trust, but the damage to their reputation had already been done.
  Lesson: In the event of a breach or crisis, transparency with clients and swift, decisive action are essential to maintaining or regaining trust.

- **Security is Never Absolute**: Even the most advanced security solutions, like RSA's SecurID tokens, are never completely invulnerable. Hackers found a way in, proving that no system is foolproof.
  Lesson: Security is an ongoing process, not a one-time solution. Constantly update, test, and improve your security protocols to stay ahead of evolving threats.

Cybersecurity Relevance: RSA, the big shots in the security racket, thought they were untouchable. But guess what? They let their guard down and got hit. It's like a mob boss thinking his turf is safe while someone's slipping in through the back door. Their SecurID tokens were supposed to be the crown jewels, but hackers made off with the loot. Lesson here is that in cybersecurity, you ain't never invincible. Constant vigilance is the name of the game.

Now, lend me your ears, 'cause this yarn ain't just about some high-tech outfit gettin' their pockets picked. It's a stark reminder that in this racket, whether you're peddlin' hooch or guardin' digital treasures, you gotta stay true to your core values. RSA had a sacred duty to protect what they held dear, the security and trust of their clientele. But somewhere along the cobblestone roads, they dropped the ball, and it cost 'em a pretty penny.

In the shadowy alleys of our world, your reputation is your bread and butter, see? Once it's tarnished, it's a tough gig to shine it back up. So, whether you're a mob boss or a digital guardian, never peddle what you hold dear for some quick dough. Keep your peepers sharp, your defenses up, and your principles unshaken. That's the ticket to stayin' ahead in this game and keepin' the vultures at bay. And remember, kid, in this world of shadows and codes, it's always wise to play your cards close to your vest and never let anyone know what you're thinkin'. Capisce?

4. Bonnie and Clyde's Bank Robberies

Alright, sit tight and listen up, 'cause I'm about to spill the beans on a tale that's as legendary as the Chicago skyline, the saga of Bonnie and Clyde. These two were the real deal, a pair of wild cards who thought they could outsmart the house and hit the jackpot.

The Spree:

Bonnie and Clyde, see, they had a taste for the fast life and faster money. They were hittin' banks like there's no tomorrow, grabbin' the dough and hightailin' it before the coppers could catch a whiff. It was a thrill, a dance with danger, and the loot was flowin' like prohibition hooch.

The Glittering Prize:

But here's the rub, for all the greenbacks they were rakin' in, they were tradin' in something far more valuable. They were sellin' their freedom, their peace of mind, and puttin' a big ol' target on their backs. The short-term gains were sweet, but the stakes were gettin' higher, and the house always wins.

The Final Showdown:

It wasn't long before the law had their number. The duo was makin' headlines, and every G-man and lawman was on their tail. The chase was on, and the noose was tightenin'. Bonnie and Clyde were runnin' on borrowed time, and they knew it. The spree that brought 'em fame and fortune was leadin' 'em straight to a dead end.

In a blaze of gunfire and glory, the law caught up with 'em. Ambushed on a dusty road, Bonnie and Clyde met their maker, leavin' behind a legacy of crime and a cautionary tale for every wise guy and dame in the game. (https://downloads.paperlessarchives.com, 1933-1935)

The Moral of the Story:

So, what's the lesson here, you ask? It's simple, never sell what you love for a quick buck. Bonnie and Clyde, they loved the thrill, the freedom, and each other. But they traded it all for a fleeting moment in the spotlight and a handful of cash.

In our world, whether you're a bank robber or a bootlegger, your principles are your true treasure. Compromise 'em for some short-term gains, and you're settin' yourself up for a fall. Stay true to your values, keep your wits about ya, and remember, the house always has the edge, so play your cards right and don't let greed cloud your judgment.

Lessons Learned:

- **Short-Term Gains Come with Long-Term Consequences**: Bonnie and Clyde raked in money quickly by robbing banks, but they traded their freedom and peace of mind in exchange for the thrill.

Lesson: Chasing fast money or shortcuts may offer immediate rewards, but the long-term consequences, whether in business, life, or crime are often much heavier.

- **Never Trade What You Love for a Quick Buck**: Bonnie and Clyde traded their love, freedom, and safety for the rush of fame and money, leading to their tragic end.

  Lesson: Don't compromise what truly matters to you—your principles, loved ones, or values—for fleeting financial or material gains. Stay grounded in what's most important.

Need a Ride? (Midjourney, 2023)

- **Stick to Your Principles**: Bonnie and Clyde abandoned any sense of security, peace, or long-term vision for the rush of their spree, which cost them dearly.

Lesson: In any endeavor, your principles are your compass. Stay true to them, and don't let temporary opportunities pull you off course.

Cybersecurity Relevance: Bonnie and Clyde, they were all about the quick score, hittin' banks left and right. But their game came with a price, exposure. Same goes in the cyber world. If you're makin' a fast grab for data without coverin' your tracks, it's only a matter of time before the law or a breach catches up with you. Cybersecurity is all about playin' it smart and keepin' your assets safe, or you're gonna end up like Bonnie and Clyde, caught with no way out.

And there ya have it, kid. A tale of love, crime, and the price of compromisin' what you hold dear. Keep it in mind the next time you're tempted to take the easy road. Remember, in this game, it's always better to be smart than to be sorry. Capisce?

5. Dutch Schultz's Attempted Assassination of Thomas Dewey

Alright, gather 'round, youse, 'cause I'm about to spill a tale of ambition, betrayal, and the steep price of chasin' the short-term green. We're divin' into the life and times of Dutch Schultz, a real big shot in the underworld, and his doomed scheme against Thomas Dewey.

The Setup:

So here's the lay of the land. Dutch Schultz, he's runnin' the streets, brewin' moonshine, controllin' the numbers game, the whole nine yards. But there's this up-and-comer, Thomas Dewey, see? He's all about law and order, and he's got Dutch in his sights.

Feelin' the noose tightenin', Dutch thinks, why not snuff out the problem at its root? He cooks up a plan to ice Dewey, figurin' it'll get the law off his back and let him keep his empire runnin' smooth.

The Fallout:

But here's where the plot thickens. The other mob bosses, they ain't on board with Dutch's grand plan. Offin' a high-profile lawman? That's askin' for trouble, brings the whole force down on ya. They give Dutch the brush-off, tell him it's a no-go.

But Dutch, he's got a head like a brick, see? He's willin' to throw the underworld's code out the window, the core values that keep things tickin', all for a shot at self-preservation. But he's dancin' with the devil, and the odds are stackin' against him.

The Final Curtain:

The mob, they decide Dutch is a wild card they can't control. He's jeopardizin' the whole shebang, and they ain't gonna let him drag 'em into the mud. So, they put out a contract, and before Dutch can blink, he's starin' down his own end.

In a cruel twist, Dutch Schultz meets his end, not by the gavel, but by the silenced gun of his own brethren. He traded his principles, shattered the underworld's trust, and it cost him dearly. (Chen, 2022)

The Lesson Learned:

What's the takeaway from this dark tale? It's all about holdin' fast to your principles and not tradin' what you hold dear for a fleeting escape. Dutch Schultz, he was sittin' pretty – had power, had respect, had a slice of the underworld pie. But he was willin' to gamble it all, to fracture the sacred trust of the mob, just to dodge the law.

In the end, he lost it all. The respect of his comrades, his standing in the mob, and ultimately, his life. It's a stark reminder, pal – never sell out your core values for a quick buck. It might seem like easy pickin's, but it'll come back to haunt ya, and when it does, it ain't gonna pull any punches.

Cybersecurity Relevance: Dutch Schultz was a powerhouse, but when he went after Thomas Dewey, he made the fatal mistake of goin' after the wrong target. In cybersecurity, it's all about knowing who you're dealing with and playin' the long game. If you try to take down the wrong system without a solid plan, you're askin' for trouble. Just like Dutch found out, sometimes one wrong move can bring your whole operation crashin' down.

So, keep your head on straight, stay true to the underworld's code, and remember – in this shadowy world of secrets and lies, your word is your bond, and your principles are the only thing keepin' you from wearin' cement shoes. Stick to 'em, and you just might make it out alive.

Chapter 11: You'll never take me alive, copper!

Let's take a stroll down memory lane, when the streets were our domain, and the law was always lagging a step behind. We had the city wired, running our empires under the noses of the "coppers" who were none the wiser. We had our codes, our silent agreements, and when push came to shove, we knew how to vanish into the urban maze, our secrets safe in the vault of the streets.

Today, the battlefield has evolved, but the war is much the same. The new racketeers are the cybercriminals, the lords of the zeroes and ones. They operate in the vast, borderless expanse of the internet, where anonymity is the cloak of choice, and information is the weapon wielded with precision.

In my time, a well-placed bribe could buy silence, and a network of loyal soldiers could secure an alibi. Now, the cyber gangsters employ advanced encryption, proxy servers, and anonymizing software to cover their tracks. They're phantoms flitting through the web, leaving behind a trail of confusion and chaos as they breach fortresses built of code.

The tools have changed, but the tactics? Not so much. We used to scout the joint, plan the hit, and execute with a mix of finesse and brute force. The modern cyber mobster does the same, only their "joints" are high-value networks, and their "hits" are executed with sophisticated phishing schemes, ransomware, and stealthy exploits that pry open the digital vaults of the 21st century.

But make no mistake, the law has upped its game too. The feds have swapped fedoras for data forensics, and their Tommy guns for trace routes. They're combing through cyberspace with digital dragnets, deploying countermeasures like endpoint detection and response (EDR) systems, and threat hunting protocols to snag these tech-savvy outlaws.

As we delve into the underbelly of cyber skullduggery, we'll uncover how the ethos of the gangster has permeated the pixels of the present. We'll see how the creed of invisibility, the art of the silent strike, and the sanctity of the secret have found new life in the circuits and servers of our connected world.

So, button up your overcoat and tip your hat low. We're about to enter a world of dodging Johnny Law.

1. The Untraceable Money Launderer

Back in the day, we had our ways of keeping Uncle Sam's mitts off our hard-earned cash. We'd run our rackets and funnel the green through joints that knew how to keep a secret. But times have changed, and so has the game. Now, the wise guys of the web are using cryptocurrency to keep their dealings in the dark. It's the 21st century's answer to bootlegging, only they're trading in bits and bytes instead of bottles and barrels.

Cryptocurrency, like Bitcoin, is the new favorite for anyone looking to do business without the prying eyes of the law. It's digital, it's decentralized, and it's as hard to trace as a ghost. These cyber crooks are laundering money with a sophistication that would make the old-timers blush. They're using blockchain technology to shuffle their ill-gotten gains across accounts, turning dirty money into digital gold.

Another day at the office (Midjourney, 2023)

Here's how they pull it off: They start by breaking up large amounts of currency into smaller, less suspicious amounts. Just like we used to swap suitcases of cash in back alleys, they're splitting their loot across multiple wallets. Then, they use 'mixers' or 'tumblers' – services that jumble up a whole mess of transactions until the trail's colder than a winter's night in Chicago.

The G-men are getting wise to it, sure. They've got their own cyber squads trying to crack the code. But the blockchain's a tough nut to crack. Every transaction is a needle in a haystack the size of Yankee Stadium. And for every scheme they unravel, ten more pop up in its place. It's a never-ending game of cat and mouse, with the cheese always just out of reach.

For the cybersecurity big shots, this means staying one step ahead of the game. They're building tools to track these transactions, to follow the money as it weaves its way through the web. But it ain't easy. Crypto's built on the idea of privacy, and that means even the good guys have to play by the rules of the game. They're learning to think like the outlaws, to predict their moves and get the jump on them before they vanish into the ether.

This ain't some penny-ante poker game; it's the big leagues. We're talking about millions of dollars in digital currency, zipping around the globe at the speed of light. And the consequences? They're real. When these cyber bandits slip up, they don't just risk a pair of bracelets and a ride downtown. They're playing with fire, and when they get burned, it's their whole empire that goes up in smoke.

Lessons Learned:

- **Cybercriminals Adapt Quickly**: For every scheme law enforcement manages to uncover, cybercriminals develop new ways to stay ahead, using services like "mixers" and "tumblers" to jumble transactions and hide their money trails. **Lesson**: Criminals will always adapt to counter law enforcement efforts. Continuous innovation and vigilance are necessary to stay one step ahead of evolving criminal tactics.

- **Cybersecurity Must Stay Ahead**: Cybersecurity experts need to stay ahead of the game, constantly developing new tools and strategies to track cryptocurrency transactions and prevent criminals from disappearing into the digital ether. **Lesson**: In a world where cybercriminals are highly adaptive, cybersecurity professionals must also evolve, using cutting-edge tools and predictive tactics to thwart criminal schemes.

- **Privacy is a Double-Edged Sword**: Cryptocurrency is built on the idea of privacy, which appeals to both legitimate users and criminals. This creates a challenge for cybersecurity and law enforcement, who must respect privacy while preventing criminal abuse.
  Lesson: Balancing privacy with the need for security is an ongoing challenge. Regulations and policies must be developed to protect user privacy while enabling law enforcement to tackle criminal misuse effectively.

Cybersecurity Relevance: The untraceable money launderer is like the old bootleggers, slippin' cash through hidden tunnels nobody could find. But now, it's digital, with cryptocurrency replacing the greenbacks. These cyber crooks are funneling dirty money through virtual accounts, using blockchain technology like we used to use laundromats. In today's cybersecurity game, you gotta track every step in that chain, 'cause these boys are making their moves as invisible as smoke, and if you can't trace 'em, you're gonna be left chasin' ghosts.

2. The Silk Road's Stash

In the roaring '20s, the speakeasies were hidden sanctuaries of illicit booze and jazz, a thumb in the eye of the dry laws of Prohibition. Hidden joints where the gin was cold and the law was nowhere. Fast forward to the digital era, and you've got "The Silk Road," the internet's answer to a back-alley dice game. This wasn't your grandma's eBay; it was a one-stop shop for everything the straight-and-narrow crowd would have a fit about.

What's your pleasure (Midjourney, 2023)

Picture this, a secret marketplace where you could score anything from narcotics to pieces that go bang, funny money to stolen goods. The Silk Road was the go-to joint for anyone looking to buy bad news. Need a hacker to crack a safe over the wires? It was a place where you could even find the services of hackers for hire, ready to do the bidding of the highest bidder, no matter how dirty the job. The Silk Road was that place, a veritable Aladdin's cave for the modern criminal.

The big cheese, Ross Ulbricht, or "Dread Pirate Roberts" as he fancied himself, ran this show like a digital godfather. Hidden in the shadows of the Tor network, a maze of secret passages on the web, The Silk

Road was his fortress, his untouchable island in a sea of narcs and badges. (Elgan, 2023)

But every empire's got its Achilles' heel, see? The feds, those gumshoes, they got wise to the game. They tracked the parcels, traced the Bitcoin breadcrumbs, and pounced on the slip-ups of wise guys who thought they were ghosting through the net. It was old-school gumption meets new-age tech that clipped The Silk Road's wings.

When The Silk Road got pinched, it was a wake-up call to the cyber world. It showed that the web's wild west days were numbered and that the feds could outfox the foxes. For the cyber security mugs, it meant beefing up their game to protect the up-and-up activities while keeping the crooks at bay.

The Silk Road takedown ain't just a story; it's a lesson for all those wise to the web's ways. It's a heads-up that even the slickest of schemes can end up in the clink. And for those still playing the angles in the shadows, remember there's always a bigger fish, and the feds are fishing with dynamite.

Lessons Learned:

- **Every Empire Has a Weak Spot**:
  The Silk Road appeared invulnerable at first, but slip-ups and oversights in its operations allowed law enforcement to zero in and take it down.
  Lesson: Even the most robust systems have vulnerabilities. It's crucial to continuously monitor and update security protocols to avoid exposure.

- **The Importance of Operational Security**: The Silk Road's downfall came from operational mistakes that led to its discovery. Ulbricht's use of Bitcoin and the tracking of packages provided just enough clues for law enforcement to

act.
Lesson: Operational security is critical. Even the smallest mistake or oversight can lead to exposure and prosecution. Proper safeguards and practices must be always maintained.

- **The Web Isn't Truly Anonymous**: The Tor network was supposed to provide complete anonymity, but The Silk Road case proved that even in the dark web, privacy can be breached.
  Lesson: The idea that the dark web or other encrypted networks are completely anonymous is a myth. Technology can always be exploited, and no one is entirely safe from being tracked.

- **Cybersecurity Must Constantly Evolve**: The fall of The Silk Road showed cybersecurity professionals that the landscape is always changing, and they must adapt to new threats while also guarding against traditional risks.
  Lesson: Cybersecurity is a constantly evolving field. As criminal tactics evolve, so must the tools and methods used to combat them. Staying ahead of the game is key to success.

Cybersecurity Relevance: The Silk Road was the cyber equivalent of an underground speakeasy, sellin' anything and everything illegal. This marketplace was built on anonymity, just like the shadowy deals we ran in back alleys. But even the slickest operations have cracks. In cybersecurity, it's a reminder that even the deepest corners of the dark web ain't truly hidden. When you run a digital racket, law enforcement's always on the hunt, and a slip-up will bring your whole empire crashing down.

Alright, let's crack this nut wide open and spill the beans on the ransomware racket that's got the cyber world by its bits and bytes.

3. Ransomware-as-a-Service (RaaS): The New-Age Mob Contract

In my day, if you wanted to run a protection racket, you needed muscle and fear on the streets. But today's gangsters? They're renting out ransomware like it's a Tommy gun for hire. It's called Ransomware-as-a-Service, and it's slicker than a greased politician.

Here's the skinny: Some brainy code jockeys cook up a nasty piece of ransomware. That's software that can lock up your files tighter than a bank vault. But instead of using it themselves, they lease it out to other crooks for a cut of the action. It's a regular business, see? They've got customer service, tech support, and even user reviews.

Take the case of the "DarkSide" crew. These mugs hit the Colonial Pipeline with a ransomware job that had the whole East Coast sweating gasoline. They snatched up the company's data and demanded ransom in cryptocurrency. The pipeline company had to cough up the dough, and it was a mess bigger than the St. Valentine's Day Massacre, see? (Vasic, 2023)

Then there was "REvil," another bunch of RaaS peddlers. They put the squeeze on meat supplier JBS Foods and walked away with $11 million in Bitcoin. These operations are smooth, with affiliates spreading the ransomware like a flu bug and the bosses sitting back, counting the lettuce. (Goldsmith, 2022)

Now, here's the rub: This RaaS business makes it tough for the good guys to keep up. It's like trying to plug a dam with your fingers—new holes keep popping up. Cybersecurity pros must play it smart, keeping their systems patched up and their guards high. They're building walls and moats in the digital world, trying to keep the barbarians at the gates.

But the real kicker is, once a business gets hit, they're marked. Paying the ransom paints a target on their backs for every other two-bit hacker with a grudge. And if they don't pay? Well, that's a gamble, too, because it could mean saying sayonara to their precious data.

Lessons Learned:

- **Ransomware is Now a Service Industry**:
  Cybercriminals no longer need to create their own ransomware; they can simply rent it out from specialized developers, turning ransomware into a business model.
  Lesson: The rise of RaaS means that ransomware attacks are becoming more frequent and sophisticated. Anyone with ill intent and some funds can initiate an attack, making it critical for organizations to bolster their defenses.

- **Ransom Payments Encourage More Attacks**:
  Once a company pays a ransom, they may become a bigger target for other cybercriminals, as paying suggests that they are vulnerable and willing to settle.
  Lesson: Paying ransom can make companies more attractive targets for future attacks. Organizations need to carefully weigh the consequences of paying vs. not paying a ransom.

- **Training Employees is Critical**: Many ransomware attacks start with phishing emails or social engineering that trick employees into clicking on malicious links or files.
  Lesson: Employee education is one of the best defenses against ransomware attacks. Training staff to recognize phishing scams and other social engineering tactics can prevent many attacks before they start.

- **Backups Are Essential**: One of the most effective ways to mitigate a ransomware attack is having reliable, up-to-date backups of critical data.
  Lesson: Regularly backing up important data can protect organizations from being forced to pay ransoms, as they can restore their systems independently of the attackers.

Cybersecurity Relevance: RaaS is today's version of renting out muscle for a hit. You don't need to be a tech genius anymore to run a ransomware scheme. You can just hire it out, like paying a thug to do the dirty work. RaaS makes it easier for small-time players to get in on the action, creating a whole marketplace of digital extortion. In cybersecurity, you gotta stay ahead of this ever-evolving game, 'cause these hired guns are growing in numbers, and they're comin' for your business.

Keep your nose clean and your systems cleaner. Train your mugs ...er, employees on the art of not getting hooked by phishing scams. Back up your files like they're the crown jewels, and for Pete's sake, don't skimp on the cybersecurity. Because in this game, if you give an inch, these modern-day mobsters will take a mile.

4. DDoS: The Digital Mob

Alright, let's dive into the nitty-gritty of the cyber world's equivalent of a street brawl: the Distributed Denial of Service (DDoS) attack. It's like when we used to send a bunch of goons to crowd the front of a rival's speakeasy, see? Only now, they're crowding a website until it keels over.

Back in the day, if you wanted to shut down a joint, you'd send a horde of toughs to block the door. In the cyber world, they do it with data packets. A DDoS attack sends a flood of traffic to a website or service, more than it can handle. It's like a thousand mugs trying to cram through a doorway meant for one. The place gets so packed, nobody can move. That's what these cyber hoods do to websites.

Take, for instance, the attack on Dyn in 2016. This was a big-time operation that took down sites like Twitter, Netflix, and Reddit. The attackers used a botnet called Mirai, which is a bunch of ordinary gadgets. like your toaster if it's smart enough, turned into a zombie army. These gadgets were hijacked to send requests to Dyn, a company that's a big shot in directing internet traffic. It was chaos, like rush hour at the Holland Tunnel, but with no cops in sight. (Young, 2022)

Not an empty seat in the joint (Midjourney, 2023)

Then there's the BBC getting hit on New Year's Eve 2015. These cyber goons didn't just throw a few punches; they went for a knockout, trying to take down the whole shebang with a massive DDoS attack. It was one of the largest assaults of its kind, and for a while, it put the BBC on the ropes. (BBC, 2016)

DDoS attacks are a real pain for the legit businesses trying to keep their doors open to the public. It's not just about having bouncers at the door anymore; it's about having a fortress with walls thick enough to withstand a siege.

Businesses gotta have their defenses up. Things like firewalls and DDoS mitigation services that can spot a flood of bogus traffic and divert it before it clogs up the works. They also need a plan, see? When the attack comes, and it will come, they gotta be ready to swing back, keep their services running, and their customers happy.

Lessons Learned:

- **DDoS Attacks Are Like Digital Street Brawls**: A DDoS attack overwhelms a website with more traffic than it can handle, causing it to crash, similar to how physical goons would crowd and block access to a rival's business in the old days.
  Lesson: Just like protecting a physical space from crowds, businesses need to have strong digital defenses in place to handle a flood of traffic from a DDoS attack.

- **Botnets Turn Ordinary Devices into Digital Goons**: In the Dyn attack of 2016, the Mirai botnet took control of everyday smart devices, like home appliances, and used them to launch a massive DDoS attack.
  Lesson: Any connected device can be exploited in a DDoS attack. Ensuring that all smart devices are secured and up-to-date is essential to prevent them from becoming part of a botnet army.

- **Firewalls and Mitigation Services Are Crucial**: Businesses need firewalls, DDoS mitigation services, and robust infrastructure to detect and block the flood of malicious traffic before it overwhelms their systems.
  Lesson: Preventative cybersecurity measures are essential. Companies must invest in strong firewalls and real-time traffic monitoring to detect and mitigate attacks as they occur.

- **Invest in Security Before Trouble Starts**: Businesses must proactively invest in security before they are hit with a DDoS attack, rather than waiting until they are already under siege.

Lesson: The best defense against a DDoS attack is a strong, proactive security infrastructure. Waiting until after an attack happens to build defenses can lead to costly and avoidable downtime.

Cybersecurity Relevance: A DDoS attack is like flooding a rival's joint with a mob of guys, causing so much chaos that nobody can get in or out. In the cyber world, they're doin' the same thing, but with data. Sending so much traffic to a website that it crashes. It's a digital shakedown, and if you don't have the right defenses, your whole operation could be brought to its knees. The lesson? Build strong defenses, 'cause the mob may not be on your streets anymore, but they're definitely online.

But here's the kicker... just like with ransomware, paying off these cyber thugs just invites more trouble. It tells every hood in the digital world that you're an easy mark. So, the smart play is to invest in protection before the trouble starts, not after you're already on the mat.

5. Cyber Extortion: The Digital Shakedown

Alright, let's talk turkey about this cyber extortion racket. It's like the old protection schemes we ran in the neighborhood, but instead of muscling in on the local diner, these wise guys are putting the squeeze on big-time corporations and ma-and-pa online shops alike.

What's your company worth? (Midjourney, 2023)

Here's how the game is played: these cyber hoods find a way into a company's system, see? Maybe they use a phishing scam, which is like conning the door guy into giving you the keys to the joint. Once they're in, they snatch up all the confidential files, business secrets, customer information, you name it. Then they drop the bomb: Pay up, or we spill your guts all over the front page of the Daily News.

Take the Hollywood Presbyterian Medical Center in 2016. These guys got hit with a ransomware attack that locked up their whole system. The hospital couldn't access patient records, couldn't do CT scans, nothing. The crooks wanted 17 grand in Bitcoin to give back control. It was a real mess—patients diverted, doctors in a flap, the whole shebang. (Winton, 2016)

Or look at Garmin in 2020. They provide GPS and other techy stuff, right? Well, they got hit with a ransomware attack that took down their services, including those fancy flight navigation tools. The word on the street is they paid a hefty sum to get their systems back online. It was like paying off the biggest, baddest guy on the block to keep the peace. (Mitnick Security, 2020)

Here's the skinny on why this matters: Cyber extortion shows that these modern-day gangsters are getting smarter and bolder. They're not just picking pockets; they're going after the whole safe. And once they've got your goods, they can bleed you dry.

So what's a business to do? First off, you gotta be wise to the game. Train your crew to spot a scam from a mile away. Keep your systems locked up tighter than Alcatraz. Regularly back up all your data in a secure spot so if these goons come knocking, you can tell 'em to take a hike.

And let's not forget about the coppers, the law enforcement and cybersecurity experts. You gotta work with these guys, keep 'em in the loop. They've got the know-how to track these rats down and the clout to put 'em away.

But remember, kid, once you're in the sights of these cyber bandits, they'll keep coming back for more unless you shore up your defenses. It's a war out there, and the only way to win is to stay one step ahead of the game. Keep your friends close, your enemies on a list, and never let 'em see you sweat.

Lessons Learned:

- **Cyber Extortion is the New Protection Racket:** Just like old-school mobsters demanding protection money, cybercriminals are now extorting businesses by locking up their systems or threatening to leak sensitive data.

Lesson: Cyber extortion is a modern form of intimidation and control. Businesses need to recognize that they are vulnerable and prepare accordingly by securing their data and systems.

- **Cybercriminals are Targeting All Sizes of Businesses:** Whether it's a small business or a large corporation like Garmin, cyber extortionists don't discriminate. They target anyone who they think will pay.
  Lesson: No business is too small or too large to become a victim of cyber extortion. All organizations must invest in cybersecurity to prevent attacks and mitigate risks.

- **Employee Training is Key to Prevention:** Many cyber extortion schemes begin with phishing scams or other social engineering tactics. Training employees to recognize these threats can stop an attack before it begins.
  Lesson: Human error is often the weak link in cybersecurity. Training staff to identify and avoid phishing scams is one of the most effective ways to prevent cyber extortion attacks.

- **Data Backups Are Crucial:** One of the best defenses against ransomware attacks is to have regular, secure backups of all critical data. This way, even if a system is compromised, businesses can restore operations without paying a ransom.
  Lesson: Regularly backing up data to secure locations is a critical component of any defense strategy against ransomware. Having reliable backups can prevent businesses from being forced into paying extortionists.

Cybersecurity Relevance: Cyber extortion is the modern-day protection racket. Back in the day, we'd demand businesses pay us to keep 'em safe, or else. Today, cybercriminals are doin' the same thing with ransomware, lockin' down systems and demanding payment to release 'em. If your security's weak, they'll take advantage, and if you pay, you'll only encourage more attacks. In cybersecurity, it's all about staying ahead of the game, 'cause once these crooks have their hooks in you, they ain't lettin' go without a payoff.

The cybercrime godfathers of today are the legacy of our streetwise past. They're running the same cons, just on a new stage. The cry of "you'll never take me alive, copper!" isn't just a throwback. It's a living challenge in the digital age. As the coppers gear up with better tech and sharper skills, the game gets tougher. But one thing's for sure: the godfathers of cybercrime won't go down without a fight. They'll keep their codes tight, their firewalls high, and their tracks covered, because in this new world, the only thing more valuable than a bitcoin is staying out of the big house.

Conclusion

Thank you for joining me on this romp through the gritty streets of the old mob world and the shadowy digital underworld of today. I certainly learned a few things along the way and I hope you did too. The game might've evolved, but the rules? They're still the same. Let's break it down, chapter by chapter, to see how the lessons from gangsters of yore fit perfectly into today's cybersecurity playbook.

Key Themes Recap

1. **A Kind Word and a Digital Gun:** In Chapter 1, we learned that charm could only take you so far, see? Just like Al Capone knew how to smooth-talk his way into a deal, these hackers today, they're workin' the same angles with somethin' they call "social engineerin'." They sweet-talk folks into handin' over their valuables, but charm alone? That ain't enough. You need the muscle to back it up, whether it's a piece in your hand or a nasty piece of ransomware.

2. **Don't Keep All Your Eggs in One Basket:** Any wiseguy knew better than to stash all his loot in one place. Chapter 2 laid it out clear. You spread out your operations, see? Whether it's a mobster's cash or a company's data, you don't put all your eggs in one basket. Lansky? He learned that lesson the hard way down in Cuba, and in 2024, that CrowdStrike outage?

Yeah, it proved you can't trust just one system. You diversify, or you sink.

3. **Everyone's Got a Plan Until They Get Punched in the Mouth:** Chapter 3 gave it to you straight. No matter how smart your plan looks on paper, all it takes is one good smack in the jaw to send everything crashin' down. Ask SolarWinds or Colonial Pipeline. They thought they were invincible, until a cyber hit landed square in the mouth. The lesson? Always be ready to take a hit, and keep swingin'.

4. **All I Do Is Supply a Demand:** Whether you're bootleggin' booze or sellin' ransomware on the dark web, Chapter 4 reminded us that the economy of crime always worked on demand, see? Today's cyber crooks ain't much different from the old-time racketeers. Only now, they deal in digital goods instead of hooch. The game's the same, just the merchandise changed.

5. **Trust Is Good, But Control Is Better, See?:** Just like a mob boss had to keep his crew in line, Chapter 5 showed us that trust alone won't cut it. Modern hackers? They're waitin' for a lapse in control to sneak in. Look at that Facebook-Cambridge Analytica mess. Too much trust, not enough control, and they got burned. The key? Don't ever take your eyes off the game, or you'll be left holdin' the bag.

6. **You're Only as Good as Your Last Envelope:** In the mob, your value was in your last score, capisce? Chapter 6 told us it ain't any different in cybersecurity. You could be ridin' high for years, but one slip-up, like T-Mobile's data breach, and your reputation's in the gutter. Keep your defenses sharp, or risk losin' it all.

7. **This Is Nothing Personal, It's Strictly Business:** Chapter 7 laid it bare. Whether you were runnin' a racket or launchin' a cyberattack, it was always about the bottom line. Personal feelings? They had no place in the business. That's why hackers, like mobsters, did their dirty work without a second thought. It was always just business, nothin' personal.

8. **Keep Your Friends Close, But Your Enemies Closer:** Chapter 8 dove into the value of playin' your cards right with both your rivals and your allies. Lucky Luciano mastered this in the mob world, and today's cybersecurity pros? They gotta do the same. You keep a close eye on your friends, but you watch your enemies even closer.

9. **Don't Let Anyone Know What You're Thinking:** The key to power? Secrecy. Chapter 9 showed that, just like the old mob bosses planned their moves in the shadows, cybercriminals relied on keepin' their intentions hidden. The second you show your hand, you're vulnerable. So you keep your cards close, and your security tighter.

10. **Never Sell What You Love:** Chapter 10 taught us that some things, even in this line of work, had value beyond money. For today's cybersecurity pros, that meant protectin' what mattered most—your data, your reputation, and your principles. Sellin' out for quick gains? That only led to long-term pain. Just ask the folks from the Panama Papers leak.

11. **You'll Never Take Me Alive, Copper!:** Chapter 11 focused on how the old mob tactics—extortion, black markets, money laundryin'—slipped right into the digital age. From ransomware and DDoS attacks to anonymous cryptocurrency laundryin', these cybercriminals? They're just runnin' the same racket with new tools. The methods may have changed, but the principles of control, secrecy, and exploitation? Those stayed the same.

Key Takeaways

- **Old Rules, New Players:** Whether you're runnin' a digital hustle or a street racket, the rules don't change, see? You gotta be sharper, faster, and always a step ahead of the next guy. Only the clever ones stay at the top.

- **Spread Out Your Risks:** Never put all your dough in one safe, capisce? Whether it's cash, data, or trust, you gotta spread it around. Keep your options open, or some punk's gonna come along and clean you out.

- **Be Ready to Get Hit:** Listen, in this game, you're gonna take some knocks, no question about it. What matters is how quick you bounce back. The faster you pivot, the longer you keep makin' that dough.

- **Your Reputation is Everything:** In this world, your name is your fortune. One screw-up, and you're finished. Just like back in the day, protect your reputation, 'cause once it's gone, you ain't gettin' it back, no matter how hard you try.

Here's the deal: whether you're ruling the streets or defending the digital frontier, the game hasn't changed it's just gone online. The same gangster principles of control, secrecy, and adaptability apply, and if you're smart, you'll use 'em to stay on top. Keep your head on a swivel, your enemies close, and your systems tighter than a safe. After all, in this racket, whether you're a hacker or a mob boss, the only thing that matters is staying one step ahead. Capisce? See You Later, Alligator.

Bibliography

Andrews, E. (2023). *www.history.com*. Retrieved from
https://www.history.com/news/black-sox-baseball-scandal-
1919-world-series-chicago
www.history.com/news/black-sox-baseball-scandal-1919-world-
series-chicago

apnews.com. (2023, 5 4). Retrieved from
https://apnews.com/article/uber-data-breach-coverup-
sentenced-san-francisco-
05b2ded36daf55012f03651cf2c7c931

archive.epic.org. (n.d.). Retrieved from
https://archive.epic.org/privacy/data-breach/equifax/

BBC. (2016, 1 2). *https://www.bbc.com*. Retrieved from
https://www.bbc.com:
https://www.bbc.com/news/technology-35213415

BBC. (2020). *www.bbc.com*. Retrieved from www.bbc.com:
https://www.bbc.com/news/technology-53425822

Beaty, A. (2024, 7 22). *https://www.zdnet.com/article/crowdstrike-
causes-windows-outage-chaos-for-airports-banks-and-more-
heres-what-happened/*. Retrieved from ZDNET:
https://www.zdnet.com/article/crowdstrike-causes-windows-
outage-chaos-for-airports-banks-and-more-heres-what-
happened/

Bible, P. A. (2016). *https://www.nvbar.org*. Retrieved from
https://www.nvbar.org/wp-content/uploads/Pages-14-to-16-
from-NGL_Magazine2016-5.pdf

biography.com. (2021, 05 18). Retrieved from
https://www.biography.com/crime/meyer-lansky

biography.com. (2021). *www.biography.com*. Retrieved from
https://www.biography.com/crime/bugsy-siegel

Bott, E. (n.d.). *https://www.zdnet.com/article/what-caused-the-great-crowdstrike-windows-meltdown-of-2024-history-has-the-answer/*. Retrieved from ZDNET: https://www.zdnet.com/article/what-caused-the-great-crowdstrike-windows-meltdown-of-2024-history-has-the-answer/

Brown, J. (n.d.). *https://www.historydefined.net/lucky-luciano/*. Retrieved from https://www.historydefined.net/lucky-luciano/

Bruno, A. (n.d.). *www.crimelibrary.org*. Retrieved from https://www.crimelibrary.org/gangsters_outlaws/family_epics/gambino/1.html

Campbell, D. (2015, 09 03). *theguardian.com/*. Retrieved from https://www.theguardian.com/uk-news/2015/sep/03/the-selling-of-the-krays-how-two-mediocre-criminals-created-their-own-legendlegends

Chen, Z. (2022, 12 30). *www.casino.org*. Retrieved from casino.org: https://www.casino.org/blog/dutch-schultz/

cm-alliance. (2022). Retrieved from https://www.cm-alliance.com/: https://www.cm-alliance.com/cybersecurity-blog/the-rise-of-ransomware-as-a-service-in-2022

cyberlaw.ccdcoe.org. (2016, 08). Retrieved from https://cyberlaw.ccdcoe.org/wiki/The_Shadow_Brokers_publishing_the_NSA_vulnerabilities_(2016)

Darkreading.com. (2024, July 26). Retrieved from darkreading.com: (https://www.darkreading.com/cybersecurity-operations/crowdstrike-outage-losses-estimated-staggering-54b, n.d.).

Deitche, S. M. (2019, 1 7). *https://themobmuseum.org/blog/rise-castro-fall-havana-mob/*. Retrieved from https://themobmuseum.org/blog/rise-castro-fall-havana-mob/

Eig, J. (2010). *www.chicagomag.com*. Retrieved from https://www.chicagomag.com/chicago-magazine/may-2010/get-capone-st-valentines-day-massacre-jonathan-eig/

Elgan, M. (2023, 01 30). *securityintelligence.com*. Retrieved from securityintelligence.com: https://securityintelligence.com/articles/silk-road-dark-web-law-enforcement/

Fischer, S. (2005). *https://www.ccgtcc-ccn.com*. Retrieved from https://www.ccgtcc-ccn.com/StardustSkim.pdf

Fruhlinger, J. (2022). *www.csoonline.com*. Retrieved from csoonline: https://www.csoonline.com/article/563017/wannacry-explained-a-perfect-ransomware-storm.html

Goldsmith, A. (2022, 11 11). *theconversation.com*. Retrieved from https://theconversation.com/: https://theconversation.com/what-do-we-know-about-revil-the-russian-ransomware-gang-likely-behind-the-medibank-cyber-attack-194337

GREENBERG, A. (2021, 5 20). *wired.com*. Retrieved from Wired: https://www.wired.com/story/the-full-story-of-the-stunning-rsa-hack-can-finally-be-told/

Harding, L. (2016). Retrieved from https://www.theguardian.com/: https://www.theguardian.com/news/2016/apr/08/mossack-fonseca-law-firm-hide-money-panama-papers

Henry, L. (2023, 08 08). *https://themobmuseum.org/*. Retrieved from https://themobmuseum.org: https://themobmuseum.org/blog/joseph-valachis-autobiography-reveals-mafias-inner-workings/

Horowitz, B. (2021, 03 26). *www.fiercehealthcare.com*. Retrieved from https://www.fiercehealthcare.com/tech/ransomware-attacks-cost-healthcare-industry-21b-2020-here-s-how-many-attacks-hit-providers

https://downloads.paperlessarchives.com. (1933-1935). Retrieved from https://downloads.paperlessarchives.com/p/bonnie-and-clyde-barrow-gang-newspaper-articles-1933-1935/

Javers, E. (2021). *www.cnbc.com*. Retrieved from https://www.cnbc.com/2021/05/10/hacking-group-darkside-reportedly-responsible-for-colonial-pipeline-shutdown.html

Jenkins, G. (2017, 09 27). *https://ganglandwire.com*. Retrieved from https://ganglandwire.com/dean-obanion-death-flower-shop/

Kassner, M. (2015, 02 02). *www.zdnet.com*. Retrieved from https://www.zdnet.com/article/anatomy-of-the-target-data-breach-missed-opportunities-and-lessons-learned/

Kavieff, P. R. (n.d.). *www.loststory.net*. Retrieved from https://www.loststory.net/history/detroits-infamous-purple-gang

Kharpal, A. (2016, 03 29). *www.cnbc.com*. Retrieved from https://www.cnbc.com/2016/03/29/apple-vs-fbi-all-you-need-to-know.html

Krebs, B. (2022, 07 26). *https://krebsonsecurity.com/*. Retrieved from https://krebsonsecurity.com/2022/07/a-retrospective-on-the-2015-ashley-madison-breach/

Midjourney. (2023). Retrieved from www.midjourney.com - Midjourney (V5) [Text-to-image]: https://www.midjourney.com/

Mitnick Security. (2020, 07 31). *https://www.mitnicksecurity.com/*. Retrieved from https://www.mitnicksecurity.com/: https://www.mitnicksecurity.com/blog/2020-garmin-ransomware-attack

Morrison, S. (2021, 06 10). *www.vox.com*. Retrieved from https://www.vox.com/recode/2021/6/1/22463179/jbs-foods-ransomware-attack-meat-hackers

Oladimeji, S., & Kerner, S. M. (2023). Retrieved from https://www.techtarget.com/whatis/feature/SolarWinds-hack-explained-Everything-you-need-to-know

Ouseley, W. (2010, 4 22). *https://www.sos.mo.gov/archives/presentations/default/kcrif am*. Retrieved from https://www.sos.mo.gov/archives/presentations/default/kcrif am.

Perlroth, N., Tsang, A., & Satariano, A. (2018, 11 30). *www.nytimes.com*. Retrieved from https://www.nytimes.com/2018/11/30/business/marriott-data-breach.html

PETERS, J. (2013, 11 14). *https://slate.com/*. Retrieved from https://slate.com/news-and-politics/2013/11/apalachin-meeting-on-this-day-in-1957-the-fbi-finally-had-to-admit-that-the-mafia-existed.html

Peterson, A. (2014, 12 18). *https://www.washingtonpost.com/news/the-switch/wp/2014/12/18/the-sony-pictures-hack-explained/*. Retrieved from https://www.washingtonpost.com/news/the-switch/wp/2014/12/18/the-sony-pictures-hack-explained/

Powell, O. (2023, 01 26). *www.cshub.com*. Retrieved from https://www.cshub.com/attacks/news/iotw-hackers-steal-the-data-of-37-million-t-mobile-customers

Roman, I. (2023). *www.history.com*. Retrieved from https://www.history.com/news/1978-lufthansa-heist-jfk-henry-hill-goodfellas

Romano, M. L. (2007). *www.bestofsicily.com*. Retrieved from http://www.bestofsicily.com/mag/art257.htm

SAMUELSON, H. (2022, 05 01). *www.chicagohistory.org*. Retrieved from https://www.chicagohistory.org/teamsters/

Schiffer, A. (2017, 07 21). *www.washingtonpost.com*. Retrieved from https://www.washingtonpost.com/news/innovations/wp/2017/07/21/how-a-fish-tank-helped-hack-a-casino/

Schwartz, D. G. (2017). Retrieved from themobmuseum.org: https://themobmuseum.org/blog/tropicana/

Serena, K. (2024, 8 14). *https://allthatsinteresting.com/frank-costello*. Retrieved from https://allthatsinteresting.com/frank-costello

Smeet, M. (2022). *offensivecyber.org*. Retrieved from https://offensivecyber.org/2022/06/07/we-buy-and-sell/

Smith, J. L. (2016). *https://www.reviewjournal.com*. Retrieved from https://www.reviewjournal.com/news/late-casino-skimmer-smiling-to-very-end/

Stempel, J. (2020, 11 24). *www.reuters.com*. Retrieved from https://www.reuters.com/article/us-home-depot-cyber-settlement/home-depot-reaches-17-5-million-settlement-over-2014-data-breach-idUSKBN2842W5

Temple-Raston, D. (2021). *www.npr.org*. Retrieved from https://www.npr.org/2021/04/16/985439655/a-worst-nightmare-cyberattack-the-untold-story-of-the-solarwinds-hack

Vasic, D. (2023, 07 14). *dataprot.net*. Retrieved from dataprot.net: https://dataprot.net/articles/darkside-hacker-group/

wikipedia. (n.d.). *wikipedia.org*. Retrieved from https://en.wikipedia.org/wiki/WannaCry_ransomware_attack

wikipedia.org. (n.d.). Retrieved from https://en.wikipedia.org: https://en.wikipedia.org/wiki/Numbers_game#:~:text=The%20numbers%20game%2C%20also%20known,those%20that%20will%20be%20randomly

Winton, R. (2016, 02 18). *https://www.latimes.com/*. Retrieved from https://www.latimes.com/: https://www.latimes.com/business/technology/la-me-ln-hollywood-hospital-bitcoin-20160217-story.html

Wong, J. C. (2019, 03 18). *www.theguardian.com*. Retrieved from https://www.theguardian.com/technology/2019/mar/17/the-cambridge-analytica-scandal-changed-the-world-but-it-didnt-change-facebook

www.fbi.gov. (n.d.). Retrieved from https://www.fbi.gov/history/famous-cases/brinks-robbery

www.legendsofamerica.com. (n.d.). Retrieved from https://www.legendsofamerica.com/dutch-schultz/

Young, K. (2022, 01 10). *https://coverlink.com/*. Retrieved from https://coverlink.com/: https://coverlink.com/case-study/mirai-ddos-attack-on-dyn/#:~:text=In%20October%202016%2C%20Dyn%E2%80%94a,stemmed%20from%20the%20Mirai%20botnet.

Made in the USA
Monee, IL
28 October 2024

e02dcd8d-4c68-4cab-a385-13ea6360e56dR01